C000216369

PORTMEIRION POTTERY

PORTMEIRION POTTERY

STEVEN JENKINS AND STEPHEN P. MCKAY

RICHARD DENNIS
2000

ACKNOWLEDGEMENTS

Warmest thanks to Susan, Euan and Anwyl for their generous hospitality and for letting us explore the old Kirkham cellars – their patience in the face of our endless questions is greatly appreciated. Thanks to Robin Llywelyn and Angharad Menna at Portmeirion village for their help, support and enthusiasm, and to the staff at Portmeirion Pottery, especially Jo Gorman, Julian Teed and Dawn Shufflebotham.

Our thanks to Gary Hopkins and Janet Fishwick for their forbearance throughout this project, Richard and Sally Dennis, Magnus Dennis, Sue Evans and Wendy Wort. We also thank Joan and Bob Anderson, John Bostock, Hilary Bracegirdle, Neil Braithwaite, Ian Bulman, Margaret Brian, Andrew Casey, Greg and Julie Chetland, Phil Colechin, Mike Crabtree, Colin Dixey, Janet Forrest-Mossley, Ritchie Franklin, Mr and Mrs Glennie, Adrian Grater, George Hesp, Iona Hughes, Nick Jenkins, Mark Jones, Cyril Morgan,. Diane Moss, Martyn Palmer, Margaret Roberts, Gianmarco Segato, Jo Wang, Anne Wilkinson, Debbie Wood and Jerry Woodward.

S.J. and S.Mc

Edited by Sue Evans

Pottery photography Magnus Dennis

Print, design and reproduction by Flaydemouse, Yeovil, Somerset

Published by Richard Dennis, The Old Chapel, Shepton Beauchamp, Somerset TA19 OLE, England

ISBN 0 903685 78 7

British Library Cataloguing-in-Publication Data. A catalogue record for this book is available from the British Library

Contents

Introduction

One wet Christmas in West Wales in the mid-eighties, I was looking through a selection of odds and ends in a second-hand shop and was struck by the bizarre graphics on a large lidded pot marked *Tivoli*, which was backstamped with the month and year in which I was born. I pondered it for a while and, despite the £4 price tag, decided that I could live without it. Later that evening, I thought again about the design and the imagination which had gone into such a creative, decorative pattern. I rushed back the next morning and bought the pot, proudly taking it home for a ritual wash before finding a use for it. It became one of my many 'useful pots for keeping things in' as Winnie the Pooh once said. So started yet another collection, and one to rival the already mountainous selection of Midwinter started some years before. Portmeirion, I discovered, was not plentiful or easy to find though this may have been partly due to the fact that I didn't really know what I was looking for. Gradually I developed an eye for the shapes and with the help of a couple of friends managed to secure a cheese dish, another couple of 'useful' pots and jars and a part coffee set. This began my interest in the Portmeirion factory and was the genesis of this book.

The research for this project has been exhausting but great fun and I hope this book meets the needs of the collectors of this new twenty-first-century collectable.

Steven Jenkins, May 2000

I discovered Portmeirion village while watching Patrick McGoohan's enigmatic television series *The Prisoner*, but it was not until 1985 that I was lucky enough to spend a week there attending the annual 'Prisoner Convention' and, like McGoohan's character 'Number Six', I've never been able to escape its magical influence.

Being a magpie by nature I began collecting items associated with Portmeirion and *The Prisoner* and have appeared in a number of magazine articles and television programmes often driving my vintage sixties Mini Moke Morris with my collections of lava lamps, Portmeirion village and *The Prisoner* ephemera. In 1996, I coined the term 'Portmeiriana' to describe Portmeirion collectables and am the editor of an irregular newsletter which circulates to like-minded Portmeiriophiles.

I first met Susan Williams-Ellis and her husband Euan Cooper-Willis in 1995 – I was working on a project to salvage architectural details from Liverpool's Sailors' Home to place alongside the historic mermaid railings which Sir Clough Williams-Ellis had rescued from the same building in the 1940s. Euan introduced me to Portmeirion Pottery's vast range of designs and since then I have been an avid fan of Susan's work. Despite visiting most of the United Kingdom's antique fairs and centres, I am still searching for those elusive rarities, especially the designs used on the set of *The Prisoner*.

Stephen McKay, May 2000

Part One

Birth Of The Village – Early Successes At Portmeirion Pottery

Sir Clough Williams-Ellis in Portmeirion village, 1932.

Sir Clough Williams-Ellis was a descendant of the Williams and the Ellis', two wealthy land-owning dynasties with roots firmly bedded in North Welsh soil. The fourth of six sons, Clough was born on May 28th 1883, in the rectory at Gayton, Northamptonshire. Christened Bertram Clough Williams-Ellis he chose to be called by the old family name of Clough. His father, John Clough Williams-Ellis had retired to Gayton after giving up a Cambridge Fellowship upon his marriage to Mabel Greaves – at that time College Fellowships could not be held after marriage.

While still a young boy, Sir Clough and his family moved to Glasfryn in Caernarvonshire where, as he watched his new home being remodelled by his father and discovered beauty in the bleak Welsh countryside while on walks with his mother, he showed his first real interest in architecture. After a happy childhood in Wales, riding ponies through the mountains and sailing and hunting with his father on the family estate, Sir Clough went up to Cambridge University to study mathematics and statistics. However, he soon discovered his true vocation and left college with the intention of becoming an architect, although this was a profession for which he had little training. He was given the use of an office in the architect's practice of A.H. Clough (his second cousin), and began to learn his trade.

In 1908, at the age of twenty-five, Sir Clough's father gave him Plas Brondanw, an old family property which was to be his home for the next seventy years. Sir Clough joined the Welsh Guards at the outbreak of the Great War in 1914 and finished his military service as a Major in the newly-formed Tank Corps. On the 31st July 1915, he married Amabel – daughter of publisher and influential political figure St. Loe Strachey – whom he had met when at an architectural conference at her father's house before the war. For their wedding gift, the couple chose the construction of a folly near Plas Brondanw. During the war, as a diversion from the horror and destruction, Sir Clough had spent his spare time making plans for an ideal miniature village. When the war ended he did not want to remain in Germany as part of an army of occupation, and instead found a London-based government position alongside his old friend Lawrence Weaver.

Between his many new responsibilities, Sir Clough began looking for 'an unspoiled, romantic setting for his dream village'. A keen sailor, he visited a number of islands around Britain and even considered a site in New Zealand, but the cost of developing in such an isolated location was prohibitive. Fortuitously, Sir Clough was asked by his uncle if he knew anyone who would care to buy the Aberia estate (from the Welsh Aber Ia: Cold River Mouth). Aberia was only five miles from Plas Brondanw, surrounded on three sides by Y Gwyllt (The Wilds), and Clough recognised the landscape of cliffs, valleys, plateaux and pinnacles as an ideal setting for his village, and also a sheltered harbour for his boat. He bought the estate and purchased adjoining property as it became available to ensure the seclusion of the newly-named Port Merion: Port because it was a harbour and after Portofino in Italy which had been an inspiration for Clough, and Merion because it was in the county of Meirionydd. Over the years, the spelling changed from Port Merion to the more correct Portmeirion and the Welsh Porthmeirion. Clough's project had to be self-financing as his architectural commissions could not sustain such a grand plan, so in 1925 he began to develop the estate and its buildings into a resort which was amusing and cheaper than the south of France.

Frank Lloyd Wright and Sir Clough Williams-Ellis, Portmeirion, 1956.

During Easter 1926, Sir Clough welcomed his first guests to the hotel, formerly the main house. It opened with some cottage accommodation, the Angel and Neptune, the enlarged main building and, possibly, the Battery. (Initially the stables and coach house provided some accommodation, the restaurant came in later and The Ship Shop was sited in its present position in 1953. The gardener's cottage, The Mermaid, was converted into guest accommodation in the 1960s.) Sir Clough had adopted a classical Mediterranean motif, a bifurcated, or two-tailed, mermaid as the symbol of Portmeirion. Using the income from the hotel, the development of Portmeirion began with the construction of a series of cottages with names such as The Angel and Neptune, each providing accommodation for guests who, over the years, have included H.G. Wells, Noel Coward (who wrote *Blithe Spirit* during his stay), and King Zog of Albania. Apart from the war years when government restrictions placed a temporary halt on building works, Portmeirion steadily grew into a fulfilment of Sir Clough's dreams, and by 1974 he judged it complete.

In 1926, Sir Clough set up Portmeirion Limited, to run the day-to-day affairs of the hotel and village. He and Amabel spent many happy years together and collaborated on several projects as well as pursuing their independent careers, his as an architect and both as authors. Amabel had been appointed Literary Editor of the *Spectator* at nineteen and, as such, was the first to publish the work of Richard Hughes and Walter de la Mare. She also wrote many educational books for children including an account of *The Voyage of the Beagle* and *The Men Who Found Out* and collections of fairy tales and science fiction. Amabel and Clough raised three children: Susan born in 1918, Charlotte born in 1919 (who later moved to New Zealand with her husband where she worked as a research biologist), and Christopher born in 1921 (who joined his father's regiment the Welsh Guards and was killed in action in Italy aged twenty-one). Sir Clough Williams-Ellis died in 1978 and Amabel died in 1983.

Susan Williams-Ellis

Susan Williams-Ellis was born on the 6th June 1918, in the Guildford house of Bloomsbury artist Roger Fry. One of her earliest memories is as a one-year old crawling up the oval staircase in her grandmother's house in Queen Anne's Gate, London, where there was a brightly coloured parrot in the study. With their wild, curly, blonde hair and bright blue eyes, Susan and her younger sister were often mistaken for twins and when out on pram rides with their nurse, elderly ladies would sometimes ask for one of 'their pretty curls' which made them furious. Though precocious, Susan was considered shy and at about three years of age was sent to nursery school to help remedy this but on her first day, because she was so young, she was kept apart from the others and cried all day. Older children were given coloured chalks and paper to scribble on and Susan remembers thinking even then that she could do better. The highlight of the day was being given biscuits on tiny Japanese plates and a glass of milk at 11am.

Clough had designed displays for the Ulster Section and Yardley's at the 1924 British Empire Exhibition and the family were taken to see the exhibits. A bizarre statue of the Prince of Wales made entirely of butter didn't impress Susan, but she loved a display of Siamese dancers wearing gilded parchment costumes cut to resemble silks blowing in the wind. At the age of six or seven, Susan attended

Evening light, Portmeirion village, 1950s.

Mrs. Spencer's School in Albert Bridge Road across the river from the family home in Chelsea. It was during her time there that she realised that she had an exceptional aural memory. During an English lesson, the children were read a Shakespearean speech twice, and then asked to write it down from memory. Susan wrote fluently and would have continued if time had allowed. Later, for 'prep', pupils were asked to write what they remembered from the day's classes. Believing that she was not supposed to produce a verbatim version, Susan found the task difficult although the details of the lessons were clear in her mind. Each afternoon, the children played games in Battersea Park, but when it rained they were instead given lessons on a variety of topics by a Miss Walker. Susan thought her a wonderful teacher and remembers one particular lesson on perspective was to serve her well for the rest of her life. When she was nine-years old, she left Mrs Spencer's and remembers this as her favourite school.

When she was ten, Susan was given a tiny mongrel bitch whom she named Grettle and the little dog became the love of her life. Susan was a pupil at King Alfred's 'Modern' School and along with Ann Stephen and Charlotte, built a proper tree-house high in a large tree with a long rope ladder for access. While she doesn't remember learning much of value from school lessons, many useful facts were gleaned from the pages of the boy's comic, *The Wizard*.

Susan's art appreciation began at an early age: at about six she remembers Cherry, her nursery governess, showing her a sepia reproduction of Fra Angelico's *Annunciation*. Later, when Susan was eleven, Virginia Woolf's niece, Ann Stephen, took her to an Italian exhibition in London where, despite the crowds, Susan managed to see Botticelli's *Venus* by squeezing through the adults' legs. Unaware that postcard reproductions were available from the exhibition, she returned home and tried to recapture the painting by drawing in pencil on a grocer's white paper bag – she became so frustrated in the attempt that she wept.

The family spent most holidays in Wales and each Wednesday there was a market in Caernarvon. It was there that eleven-year-old Susan purchased her first antique, a small mug bearing one of Dr. Franklin's Maxims, 'little strokes fell great oaks'. Her first trip abroad was in the summer of 1930 when the family travelled through Europe into Austria to stay with family friends in Wernberg Castle near Villach and Klagenfurt. The castle was dilapidated, barely furnished and staffed by just one young boy.

While at the castle, Susan began learning to swim in canals and after a few days developed serious earache. She was taken to the local hospital where she was to stay for two months, during which time she had to endure three operations for mastoiditis and was often in extreme pain. At the same time, Sir Clough was also in the hospital, suffering from pneumonia and his family were warned not to expect him to recover. A premature obituary appeared in *The Times* saying that he had died in Australia!

While in hospital Susan was given two books of photography, one of animals and the other of country scenes but remembers being so weak that she was only able to look at a page or so a day. As she recovered she began studying the illustrations in a book about the representation of knights in art and became set on being an artist when she grew up. In one image from the book, two angels are strumming mandolins at the foot of the Virgin's throne and Susan was enchanted by the grace and sweetness of the figures, and the mandolins in 'magical perspective'. She attended the Hampstead High School for Girls but her only memory of lessons is of two-period art class spent learning to spell the word 'parallel'! Susan remained determined to become an artist and her parents supported her ambition by moving her from the High School to Hayes Court, a smart boarding school in Kent. Unfortunately, the art lessons were taught by two eccentric, elderly sisters who, with closed eyes, would describe a scene, trying to hypnotise the students into painting it. On one occasion they described a laundry and Susan attempted to recreate a scene she remembered of two young ladies tying up neat parcels of washing in a laundry in Tremadoc. The sisters were not appreciative – the *Two Laundresses* by Degas was what they had in mind!

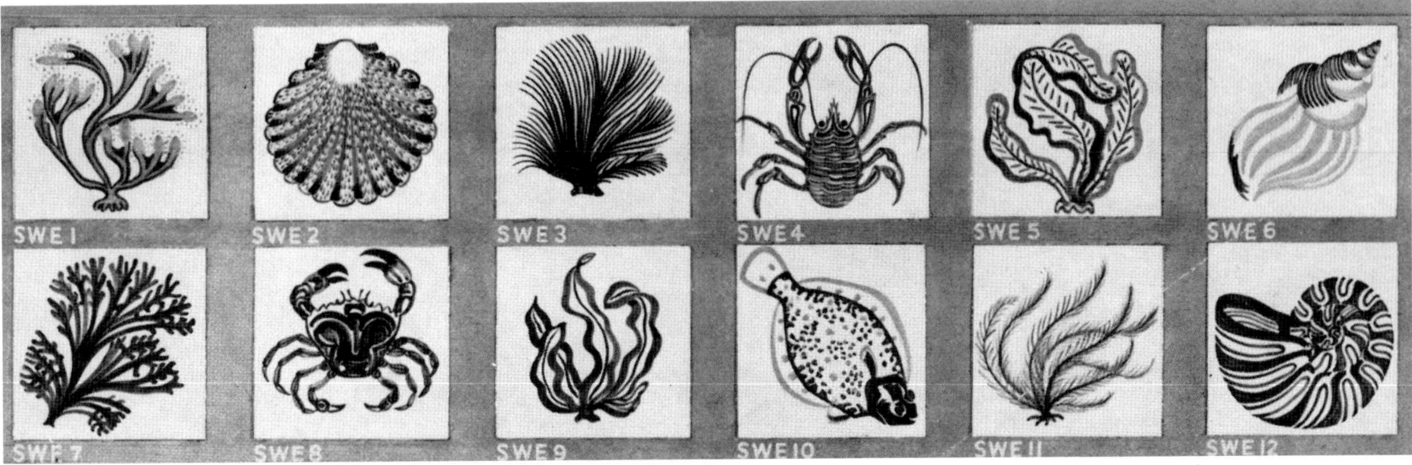

Poole Pottery tiles designed by Susan Williams-Ellis for the 'Britain Can Make It Exhibition', 1946.

Hayes Court also offered Susan her first experience of 'proper games' – lacrosse seemed unfathomable and bloodthirsty with a hard, heavy ball sailing around at head height. Her fondest memory of her time at the school was when one of the teacher's husbands delivered a van load of lignum vitae. These were ex-army mallet heads before being drilled, used by Susan to turn small lidded boxes on the lathe – invaluable practice for when she began designing and making her own pottery shapes. The Headmistress of Hayes Court, a very tall lady with several wolfhounds, told Susan that she must begin to work on her weak subjects, Latin and Maths. This, coupled with homesickness for Grettle, inspired Susan to write pages and pages in red ink begging her parents to remove her from the school. Her letters proved successful and when she was sixteen Susan went to Dartington School, a famous progressive school, where she was encouraged to concentrate on her interests, including English, biology, woodwork, art and throwing pottery; she also built a boat, painted a mural and took up life drawing. Susan was given the keys to workshops and to the extensive library and with an influx of enthusiastic new teachers, school life became bearable and even enjoyable. The pupils dug a swimming pool, using wheelbarrows to remove the red clay which was then used in their pottery classes taught by Bernard and David Leach. While throwing was of little practical use in her later career, wood turning proved a good training for making plaster shapes for block moulds (the master copy of a commercial pottery shape). Susan turned beautifully fine bowls in beech wood but these had a tendency to crack as they dried out; however, a bas relief of Neptune worked in American white wood was framed and Sir Clough cast a copy of it to adorn Neptune Cottage in Portmeirion village. After leaving Dartington, Susan wanted to go to art school at once but her parents felt that she should have a term out and stay with them in 'Romney's House', Hampstead, and attend the hated 'dreary' adult parties, where celebrities such as Virginia Woolf, Augustus John and Maynard Keynes would hold court. A very shy Susan was invariably the youngest at these gatherings and, with her cousin, often sat apart on a separate table, to avoid diluting the adults' witty conversation.

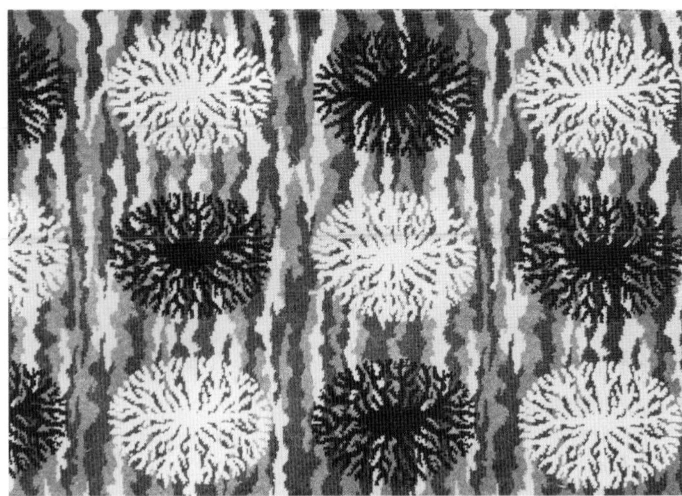

Carpet design by Susan Williams-Ellis based on mocha ware for Crossley's, 1950s.

Susan eventually attended Chelsea Polytechnic and studied for four years under a team which included painter Graham Sutherland (book illustrating) and the sculptor Henry Moore. Moore taught 'realism' classes and modelling and was a great inspiration to Susan, helping to hone her natural abilities in creating three-dimensional form. She was more committed than some of the students and made the most of her time at Chelsea. Susan bought one of Moore's coloured drawings for £12 which she later sold, together with other works, to boost the factory's finances in the sixties – 'it was the Art collection or the factory'. Unfortunately Chelsea Polytechnic closed at the outbreak of war.

Unsure what to do next, Susan returned to Wales. At the age of twenty-one, she began at Dartington Hall where

The blue drawing room in Portmeirion Hotel with carpets and curtain fabric designed by Susan Williams-Ellis.

Rug and curtains with Susan Williams-Ellis' **Music** *design, the Portmeirion Hotel .*

Susan and Euan's wedding, 1945.

she was a housemother and taught art to three- to eighteen-year olds. When the bombing started Susan moved to Soho and was employed by the Air Ministry in Whitehall. She was paid £4.7.6d a week in new treasury notes and the top-secret work was hard, with compulsory, voluntary overtime, which meant working until 4am on occasions. While Susan was working on 'G' (one of the most secret projects of the time) a member of the Air Force asked her mother, 'I wonder if she knows how fantastically secret it all is?' Susan was invalided out of the Air Ministry after developing a strange skin condition, and later began to work on exhibition displays for army education.

In 1945 Susan married Euan Cooper-Willis who had been a room-mate of her friend's brother in Cambridge. On their return from honeymoon in the Scilly Isles they moved to Glasgow where Euan was working for Blackies Publishers. They left Glasgow in 1947 with their daughters Anwyl and Sian and moved to a cottage near Portmeirion village – their other children, Angharad Menna and Robin, were born some ten years later. The family tried to live as self-sufficiently as possible, rearing pigs and growing their own vegetables. Susan kept up her artwork following her marriage, producing some tile designs which were made by Poole Pottery for use in the 'Britain Can Make It' exhibition in 1946 at the Victoria and Albert Museum. Although these were entered into the Poole Pottery pattern listings, surviving examples are hard to find. Susan produced four panels of painting for the Dome of Discovery at the Festival of Britain, 1951, and also designed and illustrated book jackets, textiles and greeting cards during this period. In 1953 she contributed an illustrated article called 'Holiday by the Sea' to the *Daily Mail Annual for Boys and Girls* and made a significant contribution to an illustrated book of seashore life which, unfortunately, was never published. In the early fifties, Susan and Euan were refurbishing and replanning the kitchens of the hotel in Portmeirion village, and Euan was also a part-time economic adviser to a firm of stockbrokers. Through a friend, Eddie Pond, Susan was put in touch with Bernard Wardle, who owned textile and plastic factories in Caernarvon and Manchester. This contact led to Susan's production of a number of textile and surface pattern designs: *Music,* (1951) a colourful design of angelic figures interposed with instruments in a number of colourways and a fairground stripe pattern in blue, pink and yellow, and *Shell Trophy,* a one-colour cotton print. *African Shields* (inspired by a dream) was a design for table tops produced on newly available fibreglass. Trays were decorated with the shell motif, and *Menagerie* and *Persian Gardens* are also wallpaper designs from this period, which may have been sample patterns. *Gala Placidia* was Susan's textile design that was selected for the new *Canberra* cruise ship. Fortuitously, rather than being paid for her design, Susan received a commission for fabric sold – when the interior of the *Canberra* was damaged by fire, a mile-and-a-quarter of the fabric was reordered, and she doubled her income!

Far right, **Hand and Rose** *fingerplate made for Portmeirion village.*

Gray's Pottery stein, c1958.

Portmeirion logo.

Grays Pottery

Albert Edward Gray FRSA (1871-1959) established A.E. Gray and Co. Ltd in 1907, as a pottery decorating firm to produce handpainted tablewares. As a pottery decorator and not a pottery producer, almost from the outset Gray's marked their wares with a bold ship or clipper backstamp large enough to cover other makers' marks, and used versions of this ship symbol until 1960.

Handpainting, floral transfer, banding and lustre finishes were the main output during the twenties and thirties but after the war Gray's reproduced many 'antique' designs, decorated with late eighteenth-century Sunderland-style motifs such as sailing ships, the mariners compass and masonic devices. 'Sunderland lustre' is a technique in which bold brushstrokes of pink or purple lustre are applied to glazed items featuring a motto or black and white engraving. Turpentine is then flicked onto the lustre as it is drying, forming a distinctive random pattern. Other motifs were used with the same lustre effects, such as *Dicken's Days* (1948), souvenir ware and engravings of country scenes by Thomas Bewick. During the forties and fifties full-colour transfers of rural scenes, sport and hunting images were popular giftware patterns. The handpainting tradition continued despite utility restrictions – floral patterns and coloured banding were still in demand and the factory had a team of highly skilled paintresses for each stage of production. However, only the more basic decorated ware or 'second quality' items could be sold to the British public until the restriction on home sales was lifted in 1953. Gray's is probably best known today as the factory that employed Susie Cooper from 1922-29 before she set up her own pottery – coincidentally, a similar career-change was awaiting Susan Williams-Ellis.

The Ship Shop

In 1953 Sir Clough asked Susan if she would like to take over the running of the Portmeirion gift shop. Initially Susan and Euan stocked the shop with costume jewellery from Petticoat Lane, decorative plates from Stoke and goods bought from travelling reps and the Blackpool Trade Fair. With the lifting of wartime building restrictions, Portmeirion expanded resulting in increasing numbers of day visitors and guests in the village, and Susan felt there should be some exclusive souvenirs available for them. Sir Clough had previously commissioned A.E. Gray to provide tableware banded in two of Sir Clough's favourite colours, pale magenta and emerald green, for use in the village hotel. (Unfortunately the ware did not survive the rigours of hotel use and commercial dishwashing – the on-glaze banding slowly disappeared). Between 1926-35 Susan's father had commissioned the Ashtead Pottery to produce souvenir items bearing the name Port Merion and his bifurcated mermaid logo.

Ashtead Potters was established in 1923 by Sir Clough's old friend and colleague Sir Lawrence Weaver in order to find new careers for disabled ex-servicemen. While Sir Lawrence was director of the United Kingdom section of the 1924 British Empire Exhibition, he and Sir Clough travelled around Europe together on fact-finding missions. Unfortunately Sir Lawrence died in 1930 and this, combined with the general decline in the pottery trade, heralded the end of the enterprise and in 1935 the factory closed.

Examples of souvenirs with the same motif as the Ashtead Potters' items have been found decorated by Gray's and may have been produced between 1935 and 1939 when the village shop needed a new source of souvenir ware. Sir Clough suggested to Susan that Gray's Pottery might be a possible supplier of small, cheap, gift items to sell in The Ship Shop. These sold reasonably well, so Susan had a copper engraving made to her own design: 'Going to Market', a traditional nineteenth-century print of women in Welsh costume was re-engraved. The items were in black and white a style which Susan preferred, or with a splattered lustre finish and made for the shop as exclusive souvenirs. A Welsh woman spinning was also used as a motif for a range of souvenirs such as tea

Hand and Rose *design, Gray's Pottery, c1958.*

A promotional photograph of **Shells**, *c1958.*

caddies, cups and pin trays, and existing Gray's copper engravings of ships and a nautical compass were produced on a wide range of shapes with and without the splattered lustre finish. These engravings proved popular and were used on a variety of coloured backgrounds and shapes well into the seventies – the masonic and heraldic engravings were promoted in the pottery press as late as 1960. The mermaid, Portmeirion's symbol, was also redesigned by Susan ready for use in 1958 (this replaced her father's somewhat risque 1920s design) on village literature, and souvenir ware included the traditional motto:

When this you see, REMEMBER ME
And bear me in your mind,
Let all the world say what they will,
Speak of me as you find

Mostly found on smaller items, the full version of the transfer showed the mermaid flanked by seahorses and dolphins. A misunderstanding at the factory led to the production of a large number of these mermaids on small, rectangular h'ors d'oeuvres dishes, an unlikely souvenir item.

Another popular decorative technique used at Gray's was 'lustre-resist'. A red syrup-like substance is applied onto the glaze to mask off an area, the platinum or gold lustre is applied and when this is dry the resist is peeled off leaving a clean resisted image. Using this technique, Susan produced a Victorian-inspired design of a hand holding a rose. As Gray's did not make their own pottery, instead buying whiteware blanks from local potteries, the factory had a varied and unpredictable level of blanks which led to production delays and occasional confusion with shapes and orders. The original manufacturer's mark can usually be seen under the Gray's 'clipper' backstamp and on many of the earlier Portmeirion items. Gray's were extremely particular over the quality of the whiteware they purchased, rejecting any imperfect pieces. While this kept down overheads, it also meant that the company had a smaller amount of ware available for decoration and the factories that supplied Gray's were less inclined to give their orders priority.

The largest transfer motif of **Shells**..

Shells

Susan has produced a great number of drawings and paintings with fish, shells and underwater themes. One of her current pastimes is to sketch underwater, drawing with grease paints on melamine board, and a television programme is being produced about this original method of producing artwork. Her distinctive drawing style is best seen in the studies of shells produced in the late 1950's for a range of Sunderland-style ware. (As far back as the late thirties, Susan and her family had worked on a book,

Promotional photograph of Sunderland lustre-style teapot, Gray's Pottery, 1958-9.

Dolphin *transfer image, c1959.*

Cornucopia *transfer image, c1961.*

In And Out Of Doors, a miscellany of activities, hobbies and crafts with illustrations by Susan.) Engravings were made of a range of single shells, fish and a small crab, varying in scale from a tiny winkle to a life-size spiny cockleshell. Working all the shells on a different scale allowed scope to find the one which perfectly fitted a lid or was the right size for the side of a herb jar. A sketch of a group of shells was intended for larger items such as jugs. Teaware in these patterns is harder to find as the factory generally concentrated on fancies rather than everyday functional items – although kitchen store jars, rolling pins and sugar and flour sifters were a mainstay. In 1960-62, the larger image of the cluster of shells appeared again on mixing bowls, and rolling pins to match, with the black print on a bright yellow ground and a gold lustre rim.

Dolphin

Susan's daughter, Anwyl, while clearing one of her mother's workrooms recently came across a number of Susan's trials and samples, including a jug with sketches in chinagraph pencil, dated 1959. The central design is an architectural motif with pediments which also form the centre of the first successful Portmeirion design, *Dolphin*. Initially produced by Gray's exclusively for Portmeirion's shops – The Ship Shop, and Pont Street, London – the design survived into the sixties on a variety of shapes and coloured backgrounds. The drawing's architectural motif is flanked by cheeky dolphins and the smaller central 'frame' contains two shells which could be cut away to add customised lettering such as 'Portmeirion' or 'Cinnamon'. Surrounding the design are swagged leaves which can also be cut away leaving only the central design for use on smaller items. Early pieces were enriched with pink lustre and known as *Portmeirion Dolphin* and usually had Gray's 'clipper' backstamp. A number were made with 'Portmeirion' in the central frame, some with traditional apothecary labels in Latin but most with the two small shells in the centre. Cheaper alternatives to the lustre version were produced on a light blue ground, or as a simple black and white print. Later, when Susan extended the *Dolphin* range she chose eight coloured backgrounds. These were considered unusual for pottery at that time but according to *The Pottery Gazette,* June 1961, 'would harmonise easily with kitchen colour schemes'.

Promotional photograph of **Dolphin**, *Gray's Pottery, c1959.*

A bright, clean yellow was one of the most successful colours – lime, grey/taupe, orange, dark green, lavender, turquoise and pink were also used with a simple line of gold lustre adding to the richness of the design. The background colour or 'ground laying' was applied to the glazed whiteware and the transfer image would then be applied. The density of the ground colour could vary a great deal, a light orange jar might look almost yellow, which may explain some of the apparently 'new' colours found by collectors, and examples are known in a deep brown and a mid green. An advertisement for the range in September 1961 offered three sizes of apothecary jars with a choice of lettering ('tea', 'coffee', 'salt' etc.), a dozen six-ounce herb and spice jars, and a rolling pin. Gift boxes were also available with combinations such as oil and vinegar bottles, cruets, pestle and mortar sets, salt and sugar sifters, rolling pin and mixing bowl, and tea caddies. In the brief 'Portmeirion Ware' period (1960-62), a simplified version of *Dolphin* was used on a range of canisters. The outer decoration and the dolphins themselves were cut away to leave a pared down image for the lettering on store jars.

During the mid-sixties much of the *Dolphin* pattern was made in a simple and highly fashionable black on a white background to suit the trend for monochrome in the home. Many of Susan's more unusual pottery shapes such as the domed jars were used as bathroom items and other kitchen shapes were also given alternative uses – an oil bottle became a cologne bottle and the sifter a talc shaker – and a traditionally-shaped shaving mug was also added to the range. In the later sixties some straight-sided jars with wooden stoppers were made with the design on the stock coloured glazes then in use, but *Dolphin* was probably out of production by about 1968.

Cornucopia

Similar in style to *Dolphin*, pineapples adorn the lids of store jars and smaller items while, on the main design, a cherry is surrounded by overflowing cornucopiae. The scroll in the centre is decorated with sprigs and fruit and perhaps the intention was to trim this design to fit differently sized items. Susan's original idea was to have the design hand- coloured but she was unhappy with the result so it was mainly produced as a black on white print, though items with green, yellow, pink and purple are to be found. One of the earliest of the new Portmeirion Ware' designs, *Cornucopia* was on display at Blackpool in 1962 but not on price lists for 1964, so production is likely to be fairly limited.

Knights

Another elusive piece of the Gray's/Portmeirion period (1959-62), is a design featuring knights. These images are inspired by commemorative plates in European churches and cathedrals where in mediaeval times through to the 1600s, a brass plaque was set into the floor in lieu of a stone effigy. The images on surviving pieces of pottery are of serene knights in full armour, produced from copper engravings in black on white or a coloured ground. Grey and egg-yolk yellow are the noted backgrounds, the deep yellow used in promotional material from the early sixties in the form of tobacco jars, beer barrels, acid dishes and King's Boxes. Most examples are gilded and from the method of presentation would seem to date from the same period as early *Portmeirion Dolphin* examples. These have not been noted on any of the shapes designed by Susan so it would seem that the pattern was not continued after 1962.

Malachite

This striking range was based on Susan's studies of the semi-precious mineral in the Natural History Museum in London. Formed from hydrated copper carbonate, malachite is found in areas of copper ore deposits and when polished has extraordinarily variable patterns. Designed in 1959, Susan's ceramic version of malachite was on display at the 1960 Blackpool Fair. Susan described malachite as beloved of the Tsars and the House of Faberge and as a symbol of restrained opulence. Historically it had been likened to mallow leaves and was used extensively in the Winter Palace, cladding walls of the 'Malachite Salon'. Susan's initial design was handprinted onto satin furnishing fabric and used in the Portmeirion Hotel. An Axminster carpet, also for use in the hotel, was made in the same design. However, production was problematic. Susan thought the early versions looked like 'chopped cabbage', so she reworked the graph pattern, handpainting all the tiny squares that represented each loop of wool in the design. She had the colour separations for the textile reduced to a scale suitable for pottery and the takeover of Gray's enabled production to take place in her own factory. The sheet transfer was cut to fit the pottery shapes and applied all over the ceramic body, rich gold lustre was applied to all the areas that were too difficult or impractical to decorate with the transfer. What might have been a production problem actually emphasised the luxurious quality of the pieces. The complete range of pottery, textiles and carpets was launched officially at the Pont Street Portmeirion shop on May 10th 1960. Susan had produced other carpet designs in the fifties – Crossley's manufactured a design based on mochaware pottery and another, used in the hotel, consisted of alternating light and dark squares, each decorated with a shell or sea creature. (Years later, when the fire brigade was extinguishing a fire in the hotel, the carpet was wrapped around a burning mattress.) The pottery range included fancy shapes such as the outlandish tureen and ladle, goblets, apothecary jars and ceramic boxes.

Decorating **Malachite**, *c1961.*

Promotional photograph of **Malachite**, *c1960.*

Moss Agate, *illustrated in* The Pottery Gazette, *1961.*

Malachite was labour-intensive and expensive to produce, and therefore sold at high prices. Some shapes with large handles and finials requiring a considerable amount of gold, made the retail cost prohibitive but Euan remembers the design being considered 'smart' in the early sixties and the public were willing to pay.

The transfer had a couple of lighter areas on it and on a plate or large flat area these showed through as almost white and spoiled the design. A teale-coloured glaze was then tried to give extra depth to the design and cover any flaws or creases in the transfer. This had the added benefit of reducing the amount of gold lustre required and eased production costs. Most items in the *Malachite* range bear the early Portmeirion oval backstamp with Gray's Pottery also credited and then the later 'Portmeirion Ware' credit. It seems unlikely that this design was in production for many years as it was so labour-intensive, but as they were cabinet rather than functional pieces, items have survived in almost mint condition. At the time of production the pottery was willing to take very small orders for *Malachite*, which allowed a shop to order a limited number and assess customer reaction. An advertisement in *The Pottery Gazette Review* 1960, illustrates the range including a goblet, oil bottle, ashtray and covered boxes. One of the later guises of the pattern was on the 'Imperial' tankard, with or without the gold lustre finish. A recently unearthed photograph of The Ship Shop in the mid-sixties shows a *Malachite* coffee set on Susan's Cylinder shape, perhaps made exclusively for the village, but it seems unlikely that *Malachite* continued in production after about 1966.

Moss Agate

While we were investigating the contents of Kirkham's cellar, we discovered a large number of boxes dating back to the early sixties. One of these contained all the sample beer pulls, tightly wrapped in 1969 newspapers, designed by Susan almost ten years before they had been packed away. We felt like true archaeologists when the unfurling newspaper revealed all the designs we had previously seen only in faded photographs. *Malachite*, lustre shells, stripes, crowns in brilliant colours and, most exciting of all, our first glimpse of *Moss Agate*. The gilding was as fresh as the day it was applied – a truly magical moment.

In London, following the reception of *Malachite* as both a textile and pottery design, Susan looked to an eighteenth-century book on geology for further inspiration. One plate showed 'landscape' or 'moss' agate stones cut into cameos suitable for jewellery, fine examples were regarded as highly as gemstones. As the mineral is being formed, small impurities force their way into the drying solution. This happens fairly quickly and inclusions solidify, creating patterns resembling hills, trees, fireworks or plants. Susan had the illustration of these detailed cameos turned into an engraving for printing and then adapted it into a pottery design. As the design was an all-over sheet pattern, it would only work on flat surfaces, much like *Malachite*, so cylindrical shapes and flat surfaces such as the King's Box (cigarette box) or Opal Box (round powder bowl) were ideal.

The production process was long and difficult: a copper plate was engraved with the *Moss Agate* design, then a hot plate was inked and a roller transferred the ink to a copper plate. The copper plate was wiped so that the ink only remained in the engraved areas. A sheet of tissue was laid onto the copper plate and the ink image was transferred to the paper, then the tissue paper was placed image down onto the glost or white ware. The paper was cut to fit the item and rubbed down to transfer the ink to the whiteware. To remove the tissue paper the item was soaked in water to leave a clean image on the ware. Best gold was then applied to the 'cameos' of the pattern and the areas that could not be decorated with the transfer. The ink image on the ware resisted the gold lustre allowing the pattern of the 'cameos' to show through. When this was fired and burnished a strange three-dimensional effect was created – Susan had invented a new technique.

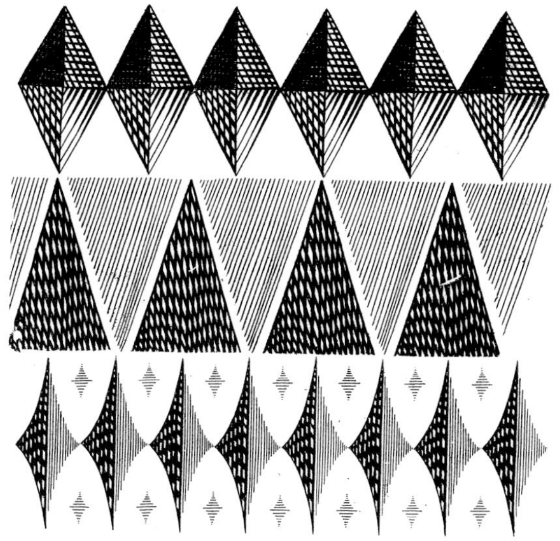

Black Diamond *transfer pattern, 1961.*

Promotional photograph of Little Town, c1963.

Moss Agate was likely to have been on display at the 1960 Blackpool Fair and is mentioned in the trade press by January 1961. Because of the difficulty in finding teaware shapes that displayed the pattern to best advantage, the coffee set was decorated on a bone-china body by Tuscan, though some of Gray's standard shapes, the lidded jars, steins and apothecary jars, were ideal for the design and were produced in standard earthenware. Among the most striking items in the range are the goblets – richly gilded and highly decorative they display the design perfectly. Another exciting find during our days in the cellar were three *Moss Agate* flat-lidded jars. In pristine condition, these seemed to us to be the finest pieces in the treasure trove. Discerning purchasers would have treasured their pieces of *Moss Agate* which, like *Malachite*, would have been cabinet pieces rather than everyday items, thus condition is likely to be good if pieces are found on the open market.

Gold Diamond

Following the strikingly different statement made by *Malachite* the previous year, when the 1961 Blackpool Fair opened many in the pottery trade were curious to see what changes had been made by Gray's new management. *The Pottery Gazette* devoted three pages to 'The new Gray's Pottery', describing it as, 'refreshingly different, reflecting an unusual and welcome new approach to pottery decoration'.

On display alongside *Malachite* and *Moss Agate* were the *Dolphin* and lustre ranges and *Golden Diamond,* a design that attracted much attention. Worked in a mixture of handpainted bronze, platinum and gold, six geometric designs formed a gift-boxed neapolitan set (different designs with a common theme) of six, small coffee cups or cans. The mix of different patterns in one set was not to everyone's taste so single items were also available. Susan had taken this idea from her grandmother's coffee set in which each cup was lined with a different colour. Strong, graphic shapes of triangles, circles and diamonds formed each of the six patterns and, as an alternative to the rich lustres and to increase production and reduce manufacturing and selling costs, a set of three copper engravings with stripes and cross-hatching was produced in the same design but worked in black on a white body. As production of the handpainted lustres was laborious and expensive a print version was formed in gold and matt black – a coffee can and saucer in this version featured in a 1961 advertisement and was intended to retail at 23/6d. Many of these early coffee cans were produced on bone-china blanks with at least three variations of handle depending on the supplier.

As the Pottery expanded and new shapes, mainly designed by Susan, were available, full Cylinder coffee sets were made in *Gold Diamond* and the cheaper *Black Diamond* from 1963. Different styles of coffee pot were available but it is unlikely that dinnerware was developed or put into production. By 1964 a price list offers only half-pint Cylinder jugs, one-pint and two-pint covered jugs in *Black Diamond* and only the two covered jugs in the gold version. For a short time during 1963, Cylinder coffee sets were available in the black and white and the mixed black and gold versions, but by 1964 the mixture of patterns was foregone in favour of one of three black and white designs or one black and gold. Items could have been made to order and Susan tried some of the *Black Diamond* design on a small Cylinder plate but this was not produced commercially. Susan's surface designs (as opposed to shapes) had been in production for about a year by the time they were on display in Blackpool in 1961 and Frank Thrower, the representative for Gray's in London and the South of England, found the response to the new ranges so enthusiastic that the factory 'had more orders than it could comfortably cope with'. Unfortunately this was a problem for a good many years. To enable the factory to increase sales it became obvious that they would need to begin manufacturing their own ceramic shapes or buy a business producing whiteware. Thus, even if factory production was slow the company had something to offer their stockists. These were put on display in the new showroom in Pont Street, London, above the antique shop Susan had taken over in the fifties. The showroom was run by Frank Thrower and his wife Inga, and the shop by Susan's cousin, Sam Beazley.

Portmeirion Ware

In the late 1950s Gray's Pottery was not an easy firm to deal with. Since A. E Gray's retirement, whenever Susan ordered or tried to get a quote for items, she was presented with 'costings' sometimes for totally inappropriate items. Once, in an effort to make it quite clear what she wished to be costed, she made colour drawings of the pieces in which she was interested. She heard nothing for months, then a large barrel arrived containing one of each of the items illustrated, but no prices. 'A letter costs 1/6d', she was told by Gray's!

Over the years, Euan had saved money from his London-based work, and he and Susan decided to purchase the ailing pottery, becoming the new owners on the 1st January 1960. When asked about the takeover Susan told the pottery press:

> I have always wanted to have a pottery, my husband was slightly horrified at the idea at first, but now is as keen as I am ...gaiety, brightness and good design are good business as well as good things in themselves.

In the early days, one of their best moves was to employ Frank Thrower, a good salesman with a keen interest in design, who left Wuidart Glass to join the Pottery. To add to Gray's slow output and to ensure that the company had items to sell, Frank went to Sweden for glass, and Denmark to buy stoneware. These ranges complemented the early Portmeirion output and helped to fill the new showroom in Pont Street, London. A turquoise oval was designed for the Pottery's new backstamp, which still had to cover the whiteware supplier's name. The wording was also changed to incorporate the new name – 'Portmeirion Ware' was born. Gray's had outstanding orders and some regular clients so after the takeover many of the old, traditional designs were still produced while Susan developed her new designs and became accustomed to being the joint chairman of a Pottery.

During this first year Susan saw the folly of buying in the whiteware and the restrictions of having little or no control over the shapes that were available. A friend of Euan's offered him the opportunity to buy a group of potteries including Portmeirion's current suppliers, Kirkham's Ltd., a producer of a wide range of ware from functional and medical items to traditional, decorative and modern tableware – Susan and Euan took over on the 1st January 1961. Kirkham's made many of the Gray's period apothecary jars and, as with Gray's, some of the original items continued to be produced. An advantage in buying Kirkham's Pottery was the virtually forgotten back catalogue of moulds and copper plates in the attics of the factory including parian jug moulds in rare patterns, moulds for all manner of strange medical items, mortars, pestles, jelly moulds and patented inhalers. As one of her first shape designs, Susan adapted an inhaler into a coffee pot.

In an attempt to improve air quality in Stoke, the Clean Air Act of 1961 declared the site's bottle kilns illegal, and gas and electric kilns had to be installed to maintain production. The staff from Gray's moved into the modernised factory and the old Gray's factory was sold in 1962. The Kirkham's site and the company were renamed as 'The Portmeirion Potteries Ltd' and the ware from this date bears the backstamp, 'Portmeirion pottery –- designed by Susan Williams-Ellis – Stoke-on-Trent – Made in England'.

Tiger Lily

Inspired by the traditions of folk art on narrowboats, *Tiger Lily* was Portmeirion's most commercial design during the 1960s. Designed to exploit the techniques of silkscreen printing, this bright, floral image was intended to have

Portmeirion Pottery display, c1963.

Kirkham's traditional shapes including leech jars.

Promotional photograph of boxed **Tiger Lily** *cruet, c1962.*

Euan and Susan, early 1960s.

popular appeal. Executed in a broad range of colours, pink roses and orange and brown lilies were set in decorative green foliage. The colours of the pattern were picked out in either pink, yellow or turquoise banding. One of the transfers was commented on in *The Pottery Gazette*, June 1961, as ambitious and possibly difficult to apply. The one concession that Susan made with the design was to use a border pattern on the plates, as it was felt that the bold central image first envisaged would wear too much in use. The pattern was rejected for display by the Design Centre in London as they didn't like the white highlights on the pattern – the darker colours show through the white and have a translucent or milky effect – although the pattern was accepted onto the Design Index.

Tiger Lily was first shown in Blackpool, February 1961, and shortly after was commercially available on traditional, bought-in whiteware shapes. An early price list shows the availability of store jars, jugs up to a four-pint capacity, a coffee pot, a range of teaware and three sizes of plate. Euan has said that dinnerware production was very limited in the early days but photographs of the full range were widely advertised and is likely to have been sold until at least the mid-sixties.

Susan has an enduring fondness for the *Tiger Lily* design and repainted it a few years ago with a view to re-issue. She even tried some old stock of the transfers on the Romantic shape but due to the continued success of *Botanic Garden* the idea went no further.

Portmeirion Rose

Portmeirion Rose was contemporary with *Tiger Lily* and worked in the same unusually bright colours. This utilised a repeat pattern of open-stock rosebud transfers alternated with coloured bands over the ware to create a modern look. As with *Tiger Lily* and other patterns, some items had block lettering for flour, salt, sugar, tea etc. It is unlikely that *Portmeirion Rose* was made in such large quantities as *Tiger Lily* but open-stock florals with simple banding were popular bathroom items, and apothecary and other lidded jars sold well in Britain and in the United States throughout the early sixties.

Blue Holland

An open-stock transfer which first appeared on the Cylinder shape in about 1963, *Blue Holland* was a traditional motif with a modern twist. Traditional blue and white bouquets and smaller floral sprigs are dotted around the ware. *House and Garden* featured the design and it became a popular wedding present. *Blue Holland* was in production until at least the early seventies but towards the end of this period perhaps only on coffee sets, although matchings for existing items would have been made to order.

London Prints

This is another design favoured by Gray's that Susan liked enough to keep in production. Some of the old engravings had a sense of fun, such as a South Seas' native smoking between decorative tobacco leaves, but the London prints were more sober and enduring. Originally a set of three, Temple Bar, St. Pauls and the Tower of London, this was reduced to the latter two. The detailed engravings were used on pink-lustred apothecary jars, trays, tankards and other fancies. One of the best uses of the prints was on the cigarette or King's Box. Printed in black on a white glazed lid and matt black body these were sometimes sold with a matching ashtray (Kirkham's round or rectangular 'acid' tray). Executive trays featured the design and were finished with gold banding or a matt black finish. Early tapered tankards were decorated with the full image or a circular cut-out, sometimes hand-finished in black. In an exciting new process developed from Susan's *Moss Agate* technique, the black print was placed onto a flat gilded surface which gave an expensive finish and a contemporary look to the pieces. This was mostly used on the boxes as the gilding could be kept to a minimum by decorating only the lids with lustre. The *London Prints* were still advertised in 1964 in black or gold but continued selling over the next few years as Susan developed her own shapes and commercial designs.

Promotional postcard, c1963.

Gold Sun

One of Susan's favourite images is a sun or star motif with curling rays. Versions are seen in drawings, trial pieces and carved motifs on *Totem*. In the factory archive a lustre resist plate with a smiling sun face has been worked in gold and a small butter pat or ashtray was also worked in black and gold as a trial piece. Working within the restrictions of on-glaze decoration, Susan developed a design utilising ground-laying and resist methods. A lustre resist image of the sun was worked in a circle and the background was worked in matt black. Gilding was applied to handles and rims if necessary and the early coffee jug had a gilded 'button' on the top. Probably only intended for coffee and teaware and small dishes, the design continued in its labour-intensive form until about 1963 when a print version was produced. In black, gold and white this was more refined and easier to produce in quantity. Mainly intended for the matt or semi matt black glaze, versions on an olive green background are known. Despite its friendly face, *Gold Sun* was not successful and faded away during the mid-sixties perhaps swamped by the plethora of decorative items bearing a similar image (the sun was an icon of the day, as was the rainbow later in the decade). Early pieces such as the beer pull or barrel, the oval teapot and coffee jug, show how advanced Susan's designs were.

Talisman

After the labour-intensive and expensive designs such as *Moss Agate*, Susan attempted a new, fail-safe approach to an all-over pattern and created *Talisman*, a design with elements that could be adapted to all sizes and shapes of ware. Drawn in black in a very energetic and free style, the rectangles, squares and circles each have a different feel, but work well together – a pattern of dots was produced to add to rims and borders. The design was screen printed, still a relatively new technique for commercial ceramic transfers. Early pieces of *Talisman* were offered in simple and cheaper black and white, or hand-coloured in blue and green, yellow and orange, pink and purple. Samples and experiments show flat colour backgrounds but these are unlikely to have been commercially produced. A promotional photograph shows some of Susan's early shapes decorated with this pattern which was first featured in the trade press in *The Pottery Gazette*, February 1962. Production was increased because it was relatively problem-free and the pattern was easy to apply. *Talisman* was well received and when orders came in Susan dispensed with another stage in production: the colour was added to the transfer in a similar, free style with a slightly off-key effect so that the transfers were now laid down on the ware and ready for firing. The loose colour background was designed to disguise small blow-holes which left white spaces in the decoration. Hand-coloured and black and white versions were then discontinued. *Talisman* was probably most popular as a design for kitchen store jars as Susan chose colour combinations which were in keeping with modern trends, but it was also produced on many shapes including dinner services and coffee sets, though these are harder to find The design ceased to appear on trade price lists in 1968 but may have still been available for matching or small orders.

Promotional leaflet, 1963.

Cylinder Shape

Susan's first designs had to be adapted to shapes bought in from other factories, but the purchase of Kirkham's allowed her to begin designing and producing her own shapes. Her love of wood-turning during her schooldays and the training she had received in Dartington School and Chelsea Polytechnic had given her a grounding in sculpture and three-dimensional design and, hence, industrial design. During her career Susan has often been told that a process won't work or that 'one should never...' but she came to the Potteries with a fresh eye and, unhampered by many of the constraints of a traditional pottery background, she broke new ground. Early designs were adaptations of existing shapes such as the eastern-style coffee pot used for the *Malachite* pattern.

Kirkham's owned many old block moulds for the sanitary and medicinal ware that they had made in previous years. Among these were items called 'porous cells', tubes that came in different widths and lengths. Susan began by choosing a cell that was the right width for the desired shape, drew a line in pencil to mark the height and then worked on a handle, spout or other feature to turn the tube into a jug, pot or cup – other shapes were carved on a lathe from blocks of plaster. Having an absolutely clear idea of what shape she wanted, she was successful at her first attempt. The sugar sifter and the cruet items had a dome top with a ball finial, and hollow ware had a clean-cut finish unlike many of the fussy edges on other teaware of the day. The coffee and teaware were the first items available and the dinnerware followed shortly after, though production of dinner services was slow until the late sixties. Other companies such as Rosenthal and Midwinter were producing straight-sided shapes and a German client asked if Susan could make an 'elegant' coffee pot. He may have been startled to see the fifteen-inch pot that Susan designed as it was unlike anything else on the market, and has since become one of the classics of its time and a popular collectors' item. The Cylinder shape was an uncompromising statement, utterly modern yet with classical and architectural influences. Inevitably the shape was much copied, but copies tend not to have the same impact as the original. Many pieces in the range have been in constant production since the early sixties, others have benefited from 'face lifts' and minor changes. As a range the tea and dinnerware was stylish and cohesive and its originality helped to secure the factory's reputation.

Black Key

A chance find in Kirkham's attic led to one of the most successful patterns produced by Portmeirion in the sixties. Susan found a copper plate with a Greek Key pattern that had been used in the nineteenth century when the motif was popular on silverware, glass, leather goods and many other items. As a pottery motif it had adorned beer barrels (many pub windows had an etched *Greek Key* pattern) and grocer's jars. Susan first applied the design to tea caddies, store jars, and early teaware items, adding bold Victorian lettering to the jars for 'tea', 'coffee', 'sugar', 'salt', 'rice', 'flour', 'raisins' and 'currants'. Marketed as *Black Key,* by the time the popularity of the design was assured, the new Cylinder shape was also in production. Susan used the *Black Key* pattern on her new coffee sets but rather than changing the scale of the pattern for differently-sized pieces, they were all kept the same and the pattern was adapted for silkscreen to increase production. The earlier copper engraving can be differentiated from the screen print version as the latter is quite flat and even, while the engraved version's pattern is formed by cross-hatching. The classical design on the elegant coffee pot had an immediate impact and *Black Key* went into full production. It continued to sell throughout the decade, adapting well to colour changes and new shapes. Substituting gold for black onto a colour created *Gold Key* on a matt white or black body, and in 1967 turquoise and orange glazes were introduced. Pink, matt lemon, lime and lilac glazes followed on a range of coffee and dinnerware. However, this series of coloured glazes proved too unstable and was rationalised to turquoise and orange. Gold on matt black was in production until 1983 while other 'fashion' colours like the matt purple (1972), and matt brown did not last as long and are likely to be harder to find. A pattern such as *Greek Key* offers the collector much scope with its broad range of colours and shapes, and a collection would illustrate the changes in interior decoration in the sixties and early seventies.

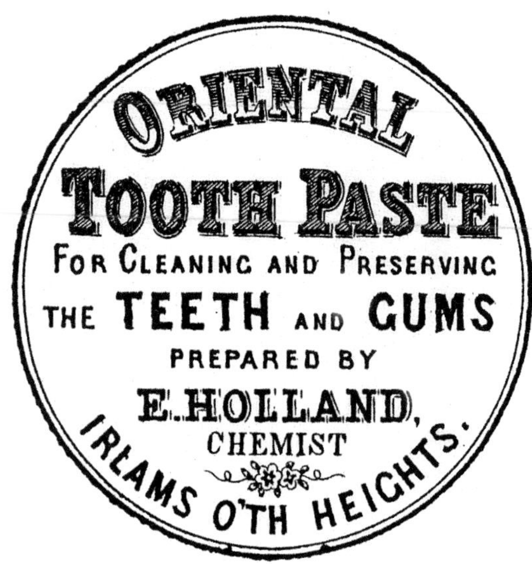

Medicine Prints

A trade advertisement in June 1962 illustrates the new range of ashtrays by Portmeirion 'taken from old (copper) plates engraved with 19th Century patent medicine titles and slogans'. These were to evolve into the successful *Chemist Prints* design that epitomised the Carnaby Street style of the late sixties. Among the range of toothpastes and bizarre products was the 'turn very slowly' transfer and a sign for the 'Universities Toilet Club', both hitherto unlikely ashtray motifs.

The early versions of this pattern were placed on existing Kirkham shapes, acid bottle stands and rectangular dishes, many of which were exported to the United States. Tankards, dome-topped jars, shaving mugs and all manner of wares were later decorated with a plethora of motifs from the back catalogue of copper plates which Susan had unearthed in Kirkham's attics. Some of the other black and white patterns had intriguing names such as *Circassian Ladies, Allan Line, Potted Game* and *Volunteers*, and appear in comany literature only briefly with some motifs appearing only on one shape, for example a jumbo cup or sifter. Designs such as the *Lapidaire Alphabet* are scarce because a retailer would have been reluctant to buy multiples of the whole range of twenty-six lettered mugs. Some Gray's period copper plates were also used, *(Mississippi) Riverboats*, a pattern simultaneously produced by Gray's and Kirkham's, appears to have still been in production in the mid-sixties.

The simplicity of producing these designs meant that they compared very favourably in price with the more difficult and expensive designs such as the soon-to-be discontinued *Malachite*. Black and white ceramics were the 'smart' interior accessory in the mid-sixties, *Dolphin* became popular as a black print and Susan found some new themes for 1965.

Country Life and Sporting Scenes

Thomas Bewick, the wood-engraver, was arguably one of the most recognisable illustrators of the late-eighteenth century. He breathed new life into the art by creating a mid-tone in his engravings, instead of stark black and white. His subject matter was informal, demonstrating his fondness for country life. Apprenticed in 1767 to Thomas Beilby, an engraver an enameller, Bewick learned copper engraving but later turned to wood. Bewick illustrated books which were reprinted frequently and his illustrations are still readily available in copyright-free form. Books such as *A History of Quadrupeds, 1791, A History of British Birds, Vol 1 1797* and *Vol 2 1804,* were the sources for Susan's *Country Life* and *Sporting Scenes* designs. Some of these illustrations had been in use as pottery designs at Kirkham's before the takeover but, combined with Susan's revived Victorian pottery shapes and her contemporary Cylinder shape, the images were given a new lease of life. The familiar oval illustrations worked beautifully when placed in threes on the body of the coffee pots, the apothecary jars resembled new 'antiques', and the gloss white pint-sized cups with an enlarged image and a matt black saucer looked stylish and modern – ideal for decoration or daily use. *Country Life* faded away through the decade but *Sporting Scenes*, now redrawn by Susan, was used throughout the sixties on a wide range of shapes, and was still to be found adorning tankards, cups and plates in the early seventies. Turquoise, matt orange and a very daring acid yellow glaze resembling lemon peel were used to give the images a more fashionable look, but a catalogue for 1970 offers only the standard black and white.

Gold Lion

Among the trial pieces in the factory archive dating back to the early sixties, is a series of Susan's designs worked in black and gold. Based on the signs of the zodiac, each image perfectly captures the essence of the star sign. Although these were not commercially produced, the lion motif, possibly inspired by the golden lion of St Mark's, Venice, was adapted into a successful design in use for ten years or more. Drawn in a distinctively free, sketchy manner the two illustrations of lions were used on a wide array of shapes. The basic lion faced right, looking fiercely forward, with his tail curling over him. The second, larger lion faced left, and is a little less fierce but more imposing. The transfer image was applied onto a matt black glaze and gilded. Cups, tankards and other teaware had a gold rim and sometimes additional gilding on the handle but the early versions of the Cylinder coffee pot had a gilded top, and a rim with broad strokes of gold along the spout and handle – quite sumptuous and Byzantine. A lampbase from this period (the shape of a coffee pot without spout and handle) was also heavily gilded but as the design continued in production the additional gilding was dropped and the simpler pattern became standard. Likely to have been shown to the trade in late 1962 and appearing in the press from early 1963, *Gold Lion* was in the price lists into the early seventies. During its latter years the lion was applied

Left, the interior of Pont Street showroom and above, Frank and Inga Thrower who managed the showroom, 1960s.

to mocha and matt white glazes in common production and the larger motif has even appeared on a matt purple executive tray c1972, and on items in the Drum shape.

The British Herald

Making its first appearance in the mid-sixties, possibly as a cheaper range, was a series of heraldic images from Thomas Robson's *British Herald* of 1830. In the days when it was always useful to know which important personage was travelling, a family's crest was displayed on the side of their carriage.

The pattern was simply called *The British Herald* and does not bear the Portmeirion name but is worked in the definitive oval used by the factory – the transfers were applied on the Cylinder coffee sets, plates and Imperial Tankards. In contrast to the Bewick illustrations the *Herald* originals were extremely fine, detailed engravings and unmistakably nineteenth century. Earliest dated pieces, such as Imperial Tankards c1966, are black on white, but Cylinder coffee sets and the Cylinder tankard were also produced on a glossy orange glaze advertised in 1970. Airtight jars with wooden stoppers were offered, as was the rarer squat biscuit jar in the same shape as the larger Imperial tankard but with a chunky wooden lid and foam recess to keep the contents damp-free. In Europe these patterns were marketed without the Portmeirion name and are occasionally seen with a simple 'Made in England' backstamp or the French distributor's mark, 'Chaumette Paris' and a star.

Corsets

A feature of 1960s style was the use of Victorian images in modern design. Susan had accidentally tapped into this with the reintroduction of old Kirkham's *Chemist Prints*. To exploit this market further, Portmeirion had to find other Victorian engravings that would provide an eye-catching, light-hearted motif. One source was mid to late nineteenth-century women's fashion magazines in which Susan found advertisements for the corset, without which any respectable Victorian woman would feel improperly dressed. Susan used advertisements for whalebone corsets such as the 'Khiva' and 'Swanbill', available from The Ladies Warehouse, Piccadilly. The full motifs included both the illustrations and the text and the rectangular motifs worked well when decorating mugs, Serif coffee ware and various shapes of store jar, and on dinner plates and other flatware.

Susan produced a large, circular design for plates, based on the female members of a Victorian family in their corsets. This, like many of Susan's black and white motifs, was later used to decorate chamber pots in the mid 1970s but apart from this, the pattern was only used on jumbo cups.

Favorite Horsemen and Pantomime Characters

One of the new sources of original Victorian designs were the character engravings from Pollock's toy theatres. Born in the East End of London in 1856, Benjamin Pollock married a Miss Reddington, whose father kept a toy theatre shop in Hoxton Street. In 1876 old Mr Reddington died, leaving his shop to his daughter and son-in-law. Young Benjamin Pollock abandoned the fur trade to which he had been apprenticed and began working as a toy maker and publisher. 'The Juvenile Drama', as the toy theatre's plays were called, had started over sixty years earlier during the Regency, as a kind of theatrical souvenir. Few new 'dramas' had been issued since the middle of the century and, by Pollock's time, this was already considered a rather old-fashioned amusement. Nevertheless, he devoted the rest of his life to making the toy theatres as his father-in-law had done before him, re-printing and hand-colouring exactly the same plays for sale at a 'a penny plain and twopence coloured'. After years of dwindling trade, Mr Pollock and his quaint shop was 'discovered' by writers, including Robert Louis Stevenson, artists, actors and politicians. He died in 1937 and, following damage in

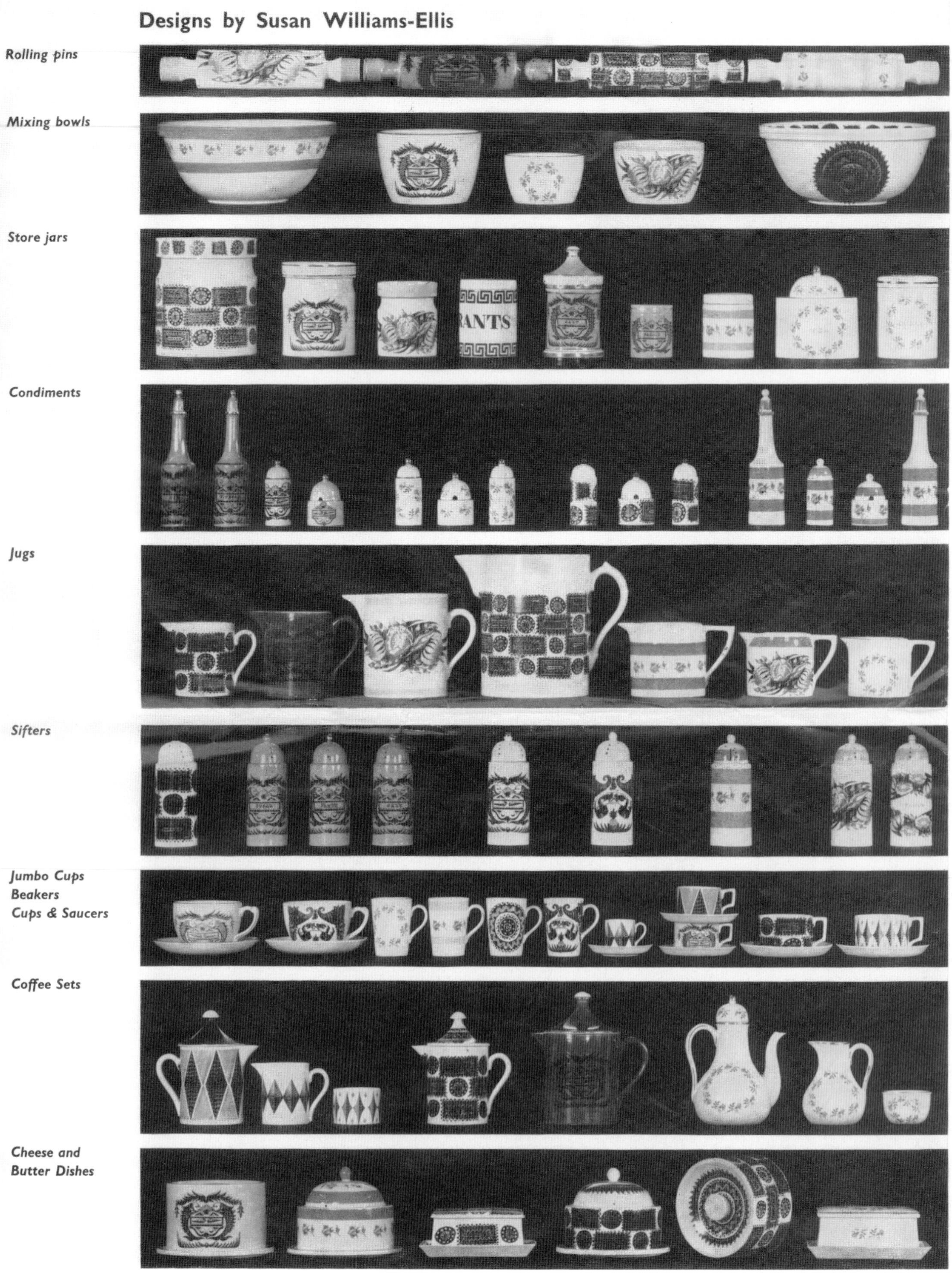

Designs by Susan Williams-Ellis

Rolling pins

Mixing bowls

Store jars

Condiments

Jugs

Sifters

Jumbo Cups
Beakers
Cups & Saucers

Coffee Sets

Cheese and
Butter Dishes

Promotional poster, c1963.

the air raids, the shop in Hoxton Street was closed in 1944. In the second half of the century, a few admirers of toy theatre got together to save the 'Juvenile Drama' from disappearance and, once again, toy theatres were restored to the shops and homes of England. In 1963 Pollock's Toy Theatres Ltd., published a short history of their company under the title *A Penny Plain and Twopence Coloured* which featured reproductions of original Pollock's engravings of *Harlequin, Columbine* and other characters from the *Harlequinade* and it was these illustrations that formed the basis of Susan's design, *Pantomime Characters.*

Pollock's original engravings had fine detail that would have been lost if converted to a transfer, so Susan redrew the characters for use as a ceramic motif. She also had to add areas of black to fill the white areas in designs originally intended to be filled with painted colours. Further research at Pollock's Toy Museum provided sufficient material for a second design Favorite Horsemen, featuring crusader knights in armour and mounted Saracens with swords raised, while the flatware featured a very theatrical Saint George vanquishing the dragon. These were produced in limited quantity but on a wide range of shapes including rolling pins and large mixing bowls. Imperial Tankards and Cylinder flatware is known but the coffee and tea items are harder to find. As the spelling of 'Favorite' on the backstamp was the American version, presumably the pattern was intended primarily for that market with more limited distribution in the United Kingdom. Both *Pantomime Characters* and *Favorite Horsemen* were also used on a range of miniatures.

Portmeirion on television

Pantomime Characters and *Favorite Horsemen* are two of the better known Portmeirion designs with sixties afficianados because of their use in the cult television series *The Prisoner* which was filmed in Portmeirion village during 1966-67. Susan Williams-Ellis was an extra, playing one of the inmates of the old people's home (in reality Portmeirion's hotel), but she is almost impossible to spot as Patrick McGoohan, the star and director of the series, asked her to keep her back to the camera as he thought her face too young for the scene.

In the episode *Hammer into Anvil,* as part of one of his many futile attempts to escape from the village, McGoohan's character uses a *Pantomime* plate featuring a pyramid of characters, to capture a stray homing pigeon. Another episode *The Girl who was Death* uses large photographic blow-ups of *Pantomime Characters* (which may be promotional items originally made for Portmeirion) as the decoration for a scene set in a record shop. Inside a village shop are rows of Portmeirion salt and pepper pots among other items and McGoohan's apartment has a *Favorite Horsemen* coffee set in the kitchen area and a smaller than usual *Favorite Horsemen* 'jumbo' cup and saucer (possibly made specially for use in the series).

Susan and Euan's son, Robin Llywelyn, the Managing Direcor of Portmeirion village since 1983, continues to commission special editions for the village shops – the Portmeirion Hotel and cottages are a perfect setting, in fact a showcase, for the Pottery's distinctive designs.

Reddington's New Foot Soldiers

Similar in style to the *Penny Plain* this design is a light-hearted look at cavalrymen through the ages. The nineteenth-century engravings were probably drawn by Mr Reddington, the founder of the toy theatre later run by Benjamin Pollock. Available in black and white or with solid horizontal blocks of red and blue as a background, this design is likely to have been contemporary with *Magic City*, designed in about 1966. It was produced for Cylinder coffee sets with an outrageous figure on the coffee pot while the jug, sugar and coffee cans are decorated with marching soldiers. Other items popularly found are the tall coffee beakers, strap-handle tankards and jumbo cups

Pantomime Characters *design, used in* The Prisoner, *1967.*

which feature a soldier firing a cannon – this image was used again in the seventies inside the chamber pots. The soldiers have also been seen marching along the top of a cigarette or King's Box, and a team of cavalrymen are seen dragging a cannon on some of the plates. When the Drum shape was in full production in the early seventies *Reddington's* along with the other *Penny Plain* and some black and white patterns were revived and applied to the oven-to-table items. Tiny soldiers or horsemen were to be seen marching around the outside of a flan dish or other cookware, and full-size transfer images were used on the inside of the items. A two-handled vase from this period (1973-75), has the soldier and cannon. The transfers are slightly greyer screen prints and differ from the versions of the mid-sixties. These can easily be identified by their shape but, because comparatively small numbers of this pattern were produced, the collector will be happy with any examples.

Sailing Ships

After taking over Gray's and fulfilling outstanding orders there were very few designs that Susan liked enough to continue producing under the Portmeirion name. Her own *Dolphin* and *Shells* patterns would obviously remain on the pattern books but from the remaining patterns few met with Susan's approval. The *Sailing Ships* range was a large selection of historic, copper-plate engravings that had been used as part of an 'antique'-style collection since the forties. An illustration of a ship or the Mariner's Compass motif would be printed with a traditional poem such as the *Sailor's Tear* or *The Sailor's Farewell* on a traditionally-shaped jug or bowl and trimmed with platinum, copper or splattered pink lustre. Similar masonic and heraldic devices were also produced in this style as seen in a Gray's advertisement from 1960 showing a full range of items including beer steins and generously-sized Athena bowls. These continued in production until Kirkham's was purchased in 1962 when Susan was able to make her own shapes. The large range of ships had a timeless quality and when the Cylinder coffee shapes were designed and in production, many of these nautical images were re-used on this ultra-modern shape and sold with matt black saucers and lids to form the *Sailing Ships* design. Each cup in the set displayed a different ship or the compass motif, and the coffee pot was decorated with six of the motifs to unify the pattern. Many variations are known: a Serif coffee pot from 1966 had a larger central image. Covered boxes, tankards, embossed plates, dinnerware and finally chamber pots were all given the nautical treatment. During the late sixties and seventies the transfers, now screen printed for speed, appeared with a fashionable turquoise background on Cylinder Coffee sets, dinnerware, store jars, beakers, tankards and bathroom items such as the shaving mug. Matt yellow and terracotta glazes are less common. In 1972 the *Sailing Ship* motifs were used to decorate Drum-shaped dinnerware available in white and blue glazes although production was soon discontinued in favour of the increasingly successful *Botanic Garden*. However *Sailing Ships* continued to be used as one of the 'Assorted Black Prints' to decorate chamber pots and giant cups and saucers until 1978 when remaining transfer stocks were destroyed in the Portmeirion fire, and the design finally retired, having been in use for about fifty years.

Miniatures

Although bedpans, bleeding basins and inhalers were not to everyone's taste in the mid-sixties, those with a sense of fun would have found Portmeirion's miniature selection irresistible. Probably taken from nineteenth-century moulds for salesmen's samples, these tiny offerings were produced for the public, not as promotional items. Jugs barely one-inch high were decorated with black and white images, the backstamp covering almost the entire base. Tiny bedpans could be used as ashtrays or, along with inhalers and bottles, cabinet curios, some of which were available with a coloured glaze finish. Pill boxes and cream pots were advertised with miniature toothpaste prints or cold cream advertisements. Difficult to find, these tiny treasures are likely to be highly sought after.

Promotional postcard, **Totem** store jar, 1963.

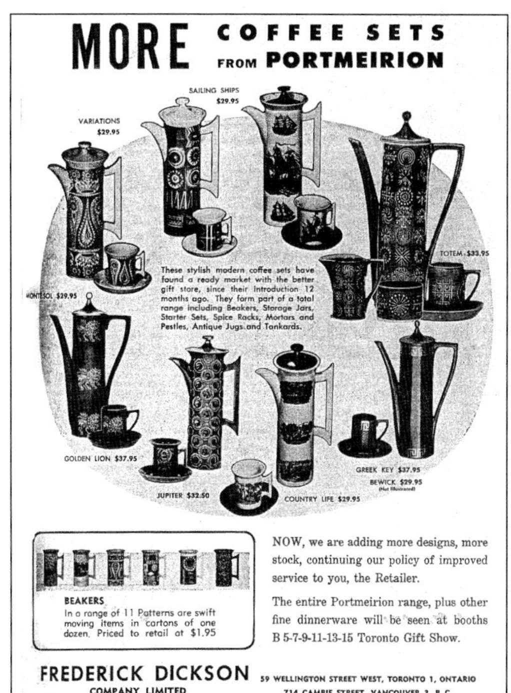

Canadian advertisement, 1966.

Totem

Once the Cylinder shape was beginning to sell, Susan began working on a new idea – if a design was integral to the shape no further decoration would be needed. This idea was ably illustrated on a nineteenth-century Prattware teapot that Susan bought in 1961. On this, the embossed areas were highlighted by an under-glaze colour; but the same idea would work with an all-over glaze forming a self-coloured design. Susan drew a selection of patterns and began to carve them into a block of plaster with scraperboard tools. When finished she took a cast in clay which was fired, glazed and from this she moved to carving directly into the pottery moulds. A variety of star-like motifs and symbols were used on all the pieces, small and regular motifs on large items, and much larger motifs on cups and serving items. Saucers would be in plain glaze colours to match. Finding a suitable glaze was a problem as most suppliers offered opaque glazes that would deaden the pattern – a transparent but coloured glaze was needed. Susan was told that the glaze colours she was looking for would run, precisely the effect needed for this design. She found a Victorian hearth tile which had

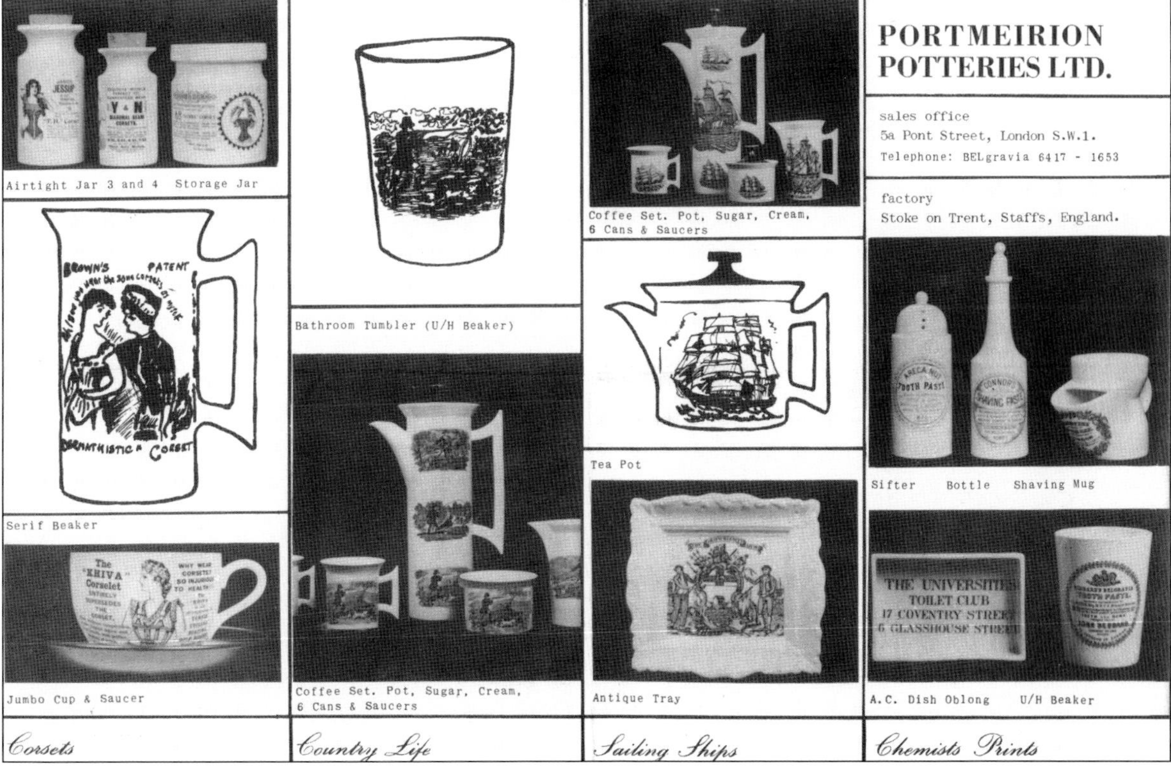

Promotional leaflet, c1965.

Promotional photographs from The Pottery Gazette *1964. Left,* **Samarkand** and **Totem** *and above,* **Totem, Samarkand** *and* **Chemist Prints**.

been produced using a 'flow glaze', located a suitable glaze supplier and tested dark green, amber and cobalt blue glazes which were just right for the design as they gave the tonal differences required. Later, a matt white glaze also gave a different look and worked well with the raised patterns. Susan needed to give the finished pattern a name, usually the easiest part of the design process, but for some reason nothing easily suggested the mystery of ancient, primitive magic evoked by this design. After looking through encyclopaedias, Susan eventually decided on *Totem*. Launched in February 1963 it attracted unexpectedly large orders, becoming the best-selling pattern of the year and putting Susan and Portmeirion pottery on the map. The pattern was seen as a major breakthrough and influenced many other companies. Though flattering, the sometimes blatant copying by competitors some of whom were better able to mass produce, left Portmeirion at a disadvantage. Inferior copies were plentiful and cheaper (often with only one or two motifs repeated to form a pattern), and while Susan's version was far better, *Totem* was ultimately overwhelmed by its competitors.

During its lifetime *Totem* was produced on the widest range of Susan's shapes, teaware, dinnerware and oven-to-table ware. An early version of the *Totem* Cylinder teapot has the shorter 'cut off' spout resembling its Prattware predecessor. A 37-piece dinner service retailed at £18.15s in 1964 and a soup set, comprising tureen and goblets cost £7.11s. Colours were added – matt white was found to show knife marks so a glossy white was substituted. Ice blue and celadon were softer options than the original bold colours but the amber and dark green versions were the favourites with the public. Susan's idea of keeping the interior of cups and beakers white against the outer colour was short-lived as workers wanted to be paid more for the 'skilled' work. A stackable range of lidded casserole dishes was made in blue, white, green and amber in the late sixties, and the oven-to-table range was available on the new, chunkier Drum shape in 1972. However, orders slowed down and eventually the factory discontinued production of matchings in 1976. (When a pattern such as *Totem* proved popular a factory would accept orders for 'matchings', replacements to an existing set, after general production had ceased. Items would very often have to be specially made to order.) Today, *Totem* is sought after both by collectors and those still using their original sets. On display in museums at home and abroad and regularly appearing in publications as a design symbol of its day, *Totem*'s status as an icon of its day is assured.

Samarkand

This Eastern-inspired pattern was worked in the same way as *Totem* but, instead of using a single glaze colour to pick out the design, the raised areas were outlined or hand-coloured. Susan chose striking colour combinations: deep blue and purple, pink and rust, blue and green, orange and yellow or purple and green were combined with black on a white background. The white body colour was changed to an amber glaze with the detail highlighted in red and black giving it a similar appeal as *Totem* – this is the most widely found version of *Samarkand*. The pattern was carved onto a number of shapes including the extravagant ice jug (a variation of the Cylinder coffee pot with a strainer to prevent ice from falling into the drinking glass) which was supplied with beakers (tall coffee mugs without handles). Store jars seem to have been the most successful selling line in the range; the larger jars with the drop-in lid were decorated as well and there are a number of trials of the covered boxes but these may not have been commercially produced. More decorative than the ice jug was the tureen which resembled a mediaeval tent or exotic fairground carousel with a ball finial on the lid. A German trade buyer observed that the soup tureen could be used as a punch bowl with a set of chalices which is how the distinctive soup goblets came to be designed. These were also carved for the *Totem* range and made in all the coloured glazes. *Samarkand* was previewed in advertisements in *Tableware*, August 1963, December 1963 and featured again in *The Pottery Gazette*, March 1964. Trade prices for the range reflect the production-heavy constraints, 55/- for a soup tureen or 25/- for the lemonade jug. A 37-piece dinner service cost £11.15s.6d which would have to be doubled to give a retail price.

Shakespeare

Contemporary with, and manufactured in the same way as *Samarkand*, a small range of giftware was produced for the 400th anniversary of Shakespeare's birth. The *Shakespeare* design was a portrait with the initials 'WS' set in a decorative cartouche and worked in high relief. This was available hand-coloured on a white background or on the green or amber *Totem* glaze colours. The range of shapes was limited to the executive tray, Candy box, large tankards and a loving cup. The tankard had an additional image of a swan (the symbol for Stratford-upon-Avon) on the reverse and the loving cup was from the same mould as the tankard with a second handle for symmetry. A price list of the time offers olive, blue and amber glazed items, also a red, and the painted option which at 13/6d to 15/- per item was about twice the cost of the plain colour at 8/- to 10/6d. *Shakespeare* was the first in a long line of commemorative items produced by Portmeirion.

Serif Shape

Not content to sit back and enjoy the success of the Cylinder coffee pot and the other pieces in her newly-designed shape range, Susan began to model a new shape. Adding a twist to the simple cylinder, Susan modelled a flaring top to the pot's tall body and the ball finial on the lid was changed to a flat, round disc (these have not fared well in use and are often repaired). The handle was adapted from a delicate curve to an uncompromising geometric shape echoing the flaring top. In silhouette the range looked like a serif typeface, reminiscent of Victorian poster lettering, and so was named Serif. Early versions of the coffee pot have a lid flush with the top of the body but this was soon revised into a 'sit-in' lid. The sharp edges at the top of the cups were softened to prevent chipping. The saucers and flatware needed no adaptation and were the same as the Cylinder versions but tureens were remodelled and their ball finials exchanged for the flat discs.

Jupiter

Continuing the glaze work begun with *Totem*, Susan designed a carved all-over pattern of circles with recesses.

Promotional postcard of **Jupiter**, *c1964.*

This was described in the promotional leaflet as: 'the concave motifs hold the rich coloured glazes in reflective pools, but at the sharp edges the glaze runs off creating an interesting contrast'. Designed early in 1964 and made available to the public later in that year, a petrol blue and a traditional Rockingham brown were chosen. The design was named *Jupiter*, its 'space-age' feel very much in keeping with the times. Unfortunately, the original petrol blue glaze reacted badly in use, forming 'oily' patches when exposed to fruit skins or mild acids and by 1966 had been exchanged in favour of a greyish blue. An aubergine glaze was trialed in 1968 perhaps to revitalise the design but this was not promoted and may not have reached commercial outlets. A full range of dinnerware was produced in the blue and brown, the plates and bowls having a single row of the circle pattern. However, coffee set production was by far the larger output, continuing until at least 1968 by which time all the Totem copies were flooding the marketplace and diluting the impact of the original.

Cypher

When *Totem* burst onto the market it was an instant success and Portmeirion Pottery was inundated with orders which generated income and allowed the factory to broaden its product range, although it was always a problem keeping up with demand. Portmeirion had made *Totem* available worldwide but exclusively for their largest distributor in Germany. When another German customer wanted to offer a similar pattern, Susan was asked to provide one. In 1963, she and Euan had been on holiday in Crete and Susan had sketched many of the exhibits in the Museum of Minoan Art in Heraklion. These prompted the idea of a pattern resembling undeciphered inscriptions and *Cypher* was born. As a glaze pattern it met the needs of the German client and the final design was made in an olive green glaze (listed as mustard) to differentiate it from *Totem*. Instead of an all-over pattern of symbols, the 'text' ran in vertical panels with deep horizontal stripes breaking up these areas. Lids and saucers were left plain and all other shapes had the pattern cut into them. British stockists were offered pewter-grey and brown glaze colours until the expiry of the exclusive contract with the German customer. Ice blue and matt white glazes were used on this design for a while but eventually the mustard became the most popular and dependable. After almost ten years of production, *Cypher* was withdrawn from price lists in 1973 – as with many other patterns, in its latter years the coffee sets were the only items available unless a special order was placed with the factory for 'matchings'.

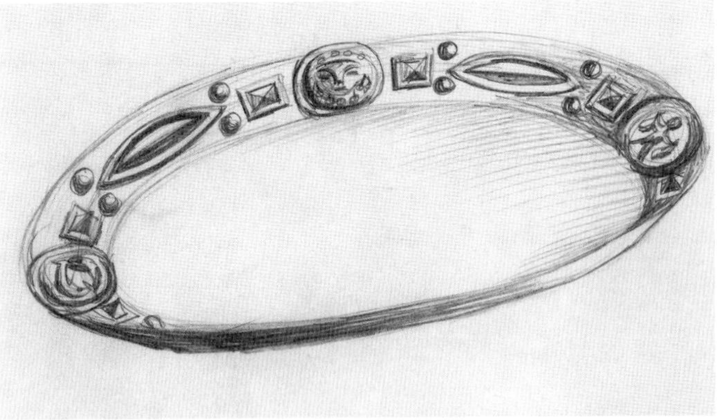

Susan's sketch for a plate in the **Fortuna** *design.*

Fortuna

Susan put a tremendous amount of work into this pattern but, sadly, it was not commercially produced (except possibly as a lampbase) – though some trial pieces have 'escaped' onto the open market, the bulk are still in the factory. *Fortuna* was possibly the most daring of all the carved designs of the period, using astrological images in medallions interspersed between boldly carved shapes and borders, an almost timeless pattern evolved. Intricate detail on all the small faces and symbols was picked out in gold lustre on a matt brown glaze. Coloured glaze versions including a bright purple and petrol blue were trialed and a Cylinder coffee pot with all the images was also made. These roundels were possibly reworked versions of Susan's designs painted on small dishes in gold and black in the early days of the factory. Examples of the lampbases appear to have been sold through the Portmeirion shop in London. A surviving sheet of sketches shows the audacity of the design, the tureen was to have a wide, button-shaped finial instead of the characteristic ball. Perhaps this was the genesis of the Serif shape. *Fortuna* would have been a very expensive and labour-intensive pattern to produce and there would have been difficulties in cleaning off the mould lines as the relief may have been softened as the raw clay was sponged prior to firing.

Jewel

Susan is pictured in a Stoke-on-Trent newspaper article in 1965 holding *Jewel*, another of the lesser seen embossed ranges. This differed from other designs in its relative simplicity. A single circular motif appears on an opal box, and is repeated three times on a lampbase (the Cylinder coffee pot without details), or extended into an oval to fit a King's Box or Executive tray. Although this has been seen with a plain blue glaze, the original concept was more striking. Rich enamel colours pick out the crescents and circles which are then outlined in gold (as are all the other raised areas), forming a rich sunburst. On trial coffee pots the Cylinder lid has been carved into an architectural form and decorated in the same way with colours and gold. Another version has a mix of two different lustres with each motif painted completely in gold and the lid decorated to match. Executive trays seem to have been the most successful shape for decorating and the finished design is highly distinctive and expressive of Susan's design work.

Variations

One of the patterns of which Susan is most proud is the early *Variations*, not to be confused with the very different and much later *Variations* on *Botanic Garden*. Totally abstract, the pattern demonstrates Susan's background and interest in textile design. She brought a fresh attitude to the industry believing there should be more crossovers between the applied arts.

Variations evolved from the idea of a sheet transfer that could be cut to fit any shape, rather like *Malachite* or *Talisman*. Susan took the size of a sheet transfer and divided it into blocks and widths that would fit different items from the Serif range. She then produced a geometric drawing in black and when happy with this, began to think about colour. Susan's method of adding colour to a

Susan and Euan showing a buyer the **Samarkand** *design, c1964.*

pattern was to cut transparent, self-adhesive film in different colours and overlay them on the drawing – a third colour was produced where two colours overlapped, adding depth to the design. Pink and brown were trialed alongside a tan and grey version and the latter was thought to have most sales potential. Launched in 1964 the pattern was available on the full range of Serif shapes: coffee, tea and dinnerware. Cylinder and Imperial Tankards, sifters, cruets and all sizes and varieties of store jars were also decorated with this clever design, its sketchy black lines cunningly disguising the occasional 'blow holes' that occurred during the firing process. Much of the factory's output during the time that *Variations* was in production bears the dated rubber backstamps with the month and year, e.g. 8/64. This seems to have only been in use for about three years as no items have been noted after 1966. This mark probably refers to the date the shape was made rather than a decoration date but it is still a useful device for the collector. Styles changed quickly in the sixties and *Variations* was discontinued before 1968, though still available by special order for replacements. As the name suggests, one of the design's most attractive features is that one is unlikely to find two pieces quite the same which must have elevated the pattern over those of its competitors.

Portmeirion Hotel wine list, 1960s.

Sketch for **Tivoli** *design.*

Tivoli

Tivoli was inspired by a visit to the Tivoli Gardens, Copenhagen. Originally this pattern was worked in pink and blue self-adhesive papers, cut by Susan into different shapes to form an all-over pattern. *Variations* had shown that using a sheet transfer that could be cut to fit any shape, was a successful idea. The original *Tivoli* 'sketch' was reworked, the details reduced in size and more patterns added to make a panel large enough to try out on a selection of shapes. The first batch of transfers were each produced in two contrasting colours, pink and blue, violet and grey, red and orange and one version in two tones of grey. Frank Thrower suggested that the simple, softest version was likely to be the most marketable, so a softer mix of blue and pale brown was produced. Turquoise and olive green was also thought to be a good mix for the pattern and for marketability. The press did not seem to promote the pattern as heavily as they had other Portmeirion designs but *The Pottery Gazette* featured the coffee set in September, 1964, mentioning other (embossed) patterns, that were available on the 'new' Serif' shape. *Tivoli* was launched in early 1964 and while it looked very stylish next to its competitors, the design never sold in the quantities hoped for. Coffee sets in both colourways were fairly popular and the kitchen store jars were even better sellers, but the pattern seems to have been in production for only a few years. Fortunately for collectors it does appear on a diversity of shapes including the handsome Imperial tankard and some Cylinder items.

Shells on Bathroom Ware

One of the rarer designs of the mid-sixties was taken from one of Susan's studies of seashells. Sold in small quantities in the United Kingdom, possibly exclusively to Liberty of London, the pattern was sold more extensively in the United States. Screen-printed in shades of greens and pinks, a cluster of shells form the central motif. A periwinkle was used as a spot motif on lids and smaller items. In style it was reminiscent of *Tiger Lily* with areas of flat colour forming a three-dimensional effect. The pattern was softened with a light pink handpainted band or occasionally a gold line to the edge of the item. Probably made on bathroom shapes rather than kitchenware the pattern is known on cologne bottles, talc sifters, apothecary jars and dome-lidded pots. Most of these pieces date from 1965 and are likely to have been superseded by the cheaper, open-stock floral transfers that were more adaptable.

Monte Sol

While breakfasting in the Monte Sol Hotel, Ibiza, Susan produced a pattern in felt tip pens. She feels she often works best out of the studio, where ideas can flow more freely. Euan and she had been very inspired by Moorish tiles and the rich colours of their Hispano-Moresque surroundings and Susan developed a pattern with a paisley motif topped with crowns and rosettes. This was worked in two colours, rich green and a deep blue. Another colourway, turquoise and lilac, also echoed the surroundings. These patterns were adapted for the Serif coffee shape with little or no adaptation from the original drawings in the two colourways. The pattern was then adapted for dinnerware with a mirror image design repeated to form a whole, stars and a stylised 'volcano' appear on the flatware design. First promoted in the press in September 1965 the pattern was probably most successful on the wooden-topped store jars and sets of six herb jars in a wooden rack. The blue/green colourway typified the current fashion and was far more popular than its paler counterpart as it suited the 'swinging' look of the day. Special 'for the kitchen' leaflets were produced with a rolling pin and mixing bowl and a set of jars with integral buttons for hanging on a wall-mounted rack. The pattern was not on the price lists for a year and at one point was announced as discontinued. However, it made a remarkable resurgence at the turn of the decade as *Marrakesh*, the name evoking the cultural aspirations of many young people who were dropping out of traditional society and taking a fresh look at the world. The Monte Sol transfer was placed on the Cylinder coffee shape and glazed in a citron (deep lime green), with black accessories (saucers and lids). This psychedelic coffee set was promoted in the 1970 catalogue and the design was unlikely to have been made on other commercial shapes. From the same period, but not thought to have been made in quantity, were striking pink glazed jars with wooden tops. Many of these late sixties brighter glaze colours were temperamental and unpredictable in the kiln and were later restricted to the reliable turquoise and orange glazes.

Mortars and Pestles

For many years after the acquisition of Kirkham's Pottery, Portmeirion continued to produce unglazed, acid proof, stoneware mortars and wooden-handled pestles. Mortars and pestles were the traditional tools of artists, alchemists and later chemists who still use this simple apparatus to grind compounds. The use of mortars to grind spices for culinary use was relatively unusual in the seventies, and Portmeirion would have sold the majority of their output to scientific supply companies. Each mortar and pestle has an embossed size number as the curved surfaces of both pieces have to match to allow maximum grinding efficiency. Unfortunately there was no maker's mark to distinguish them from any other factory's product. Ten sizes were available: No.0000 3" (7.5cms), No.000 3" (7.5cms), No.00 3" (7.5cms), No.0 4" (10cms), No.2 5" (12.5cms), No.3 6" (15cms), No.4 6" (15cms), No.5 7" (18cms), No.6 8" (20.5cms). When the mortar and pestle were discontinued in 1973, the long connection between Kirkham's Pottery and the sciences was finally broken.

Volterra *shape, as illustrated in the Stoke* Sentinel, *1965.*

Volterra

One of the most outlandish and original shapes Susan designed in the sixties, sadly *Volterra* was not commercially produced. A development of her embossed work, this shape has an eastern influence and an exceptional fluidity. A gourd-like shape tapers into a ball finial on the coffee pot and a graceful handle sweeps up and joins the base of the body, pronounced ribbing over the shape accentuates the grace of the form. The matching cups were a flared tulip shape on a slim pedestal. Thinking these would be easy to knock over, Susan designed a cunning detail on the saucer – a spike to hold and stabilise the cup! Although the coffee set was modelled and test glazes were trialed, the design was perhaps considered a little too *avant garde*, despite its practicality.

Another tall coffee pot with a flared base was modelled and trialed extensively. This, like the pattern *Fortuna*, also contained decorative rosettes at the base with ribbing on the upper body. An interesting feature was a lock-lid that sat snugly on the pot. Susan also experimented with sprigged motifs on different shapes. She bought a large barrel of these moulds from T.G. Green's factory – many

All designs are by Susan Williams-Ellis unless otherwise stated

Portmeirion souvenirs: Ashtead Pottery vase with Sir Clough Williams-Ellis design and Grays Pottery jug with a print and enamel version of the same image. Susan Williams-Ellis' 1958 version of the Portmeirion logo on fancies, and a sample 'Bermuda' tobacco jar. The Welsh engravings were commissioned from Gray's by Susan to sell in the gift shop in Portmeirion village.

Traditional prints including 'Sailing Ships', 'Riverboats' and 'London'. Sunderland-style lustre, Gray's Pottery & Portmeirion Ware.

Shells – *Sunderland-style lustre, white and groundlay colour items, Gray's Pottery, from 1959.*

Malachite – *selection of early shapes and Susan's Cylinder range, including the coffee pot which she adapted from an old inhaler mould. The covered box is a trial from Grays Pottery and possibly one of the first pieces made. Gray's, Portmeirion Ware and Portmeirion Pottery from 1960.*

As above with background fabric launched at the same time as the pottery design.

Promotional photograph for **Moss Agate**, *Portmeirion Ware c1961.*

Moss Agate – *coffee ware items on bone china, other items are earthenware. Portmeirion Ware from 1961.*

Top row left, **Dolphin pattern** *with Sunderland-style lustre finish. The central bar could be customised to read 'Portmeirion' or 'Tea', 'Coffee' or 'Sugar' depending on the shape and use, Gray's Pottery 1958-60; above right,* **Cornucopia**, *available as a black print or as a hand-coloured version, Portmeirion Ware from 1961.*

Second row, coloured **Dolphin**, *selection of shapes and colours including apothecary jars, herb and spice jars, plates, sifters, vinegar bottle and rolling pin; the pale blue conical jar is from the 1961-2 period. Portmeirion Ware and Portmeirion Pottery from 1960.*

Above left, **Nursery** *patterns, North American Indian open-stock pattern, all others Richard Doyle illustrations c1840s. Gray's, Portmeirion Ware from 1961; Above right, Kirkham motifs produced by Portmeirion, 1962.*

Right, groundlay colours – a selection of patterns found on both Gray's and Portmeirion Ware, late 1950s, early 1960s.

Gold Diamond *and* **Black Diamond** *– six different patterns made up the original set of gold coffee cans, these were reduced to one pattern as shown on the Cylinder coffee pot. The bone china coffee can on the left is an early handpainted version. Three of the gold patterns were reworked in black and used on a cheaper range of coffee ware. The black cup with white pattern and the green and black cup are factory trials. Portmeirion Pottery from 1961.*

Advertisement, 1961.

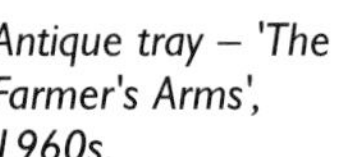

Antique tray – 'The Farmer's Arms', 1960s.

Banded ware and **Portmeirion Rose** *– the jug and herb jar are probably the same colourway commissioned by Sir Clough Williams-Ellis for dinnerware, the jar, cup and saucer are on 'bought-in' shapes. Portmeirion Ware and Portmerion Pottery from 1961.*

London Prints *– traditional images of Temple Bar, St Paul's Cathedral and the Tower of London on a variety of shapes. The dish at the front is by Gray's Pottery and the gold versions are a technique devised by Susan Williams-Ellis. Portmeirion Ware and Portmeirion Pottery from 1960.*

Little Town *– a promotional design on new shapes, c1962.*

Tiger Lily – *screen-printed design inspired by barge-ware banded in either turquoise or yellow. Many of the kitchen items were standard Kirkham Pottery shapes. Portmeirion Ware and Portmeirion Pottery from 1962.*

Promotional photograph of decorative beer pulls, c1961.

Promotional photograph for **Tiger Lily**, *c1962.*

Promotional photograph for beer barrels, c1961.

Gold Lion – *Cylinder coffee items, an apothecary and domed bathroom jar feature the small lion. The executive tray has the larger lion image. In later production much less gold was used. Portmeirion Pottery from 1963.*

Gold Sun – *produced as a lustre resist image, a transfer made production quicker and cheaper. The covered jug is an early item, the selection of wares on matt black Cylinder shapes are later. Portmeirion Ware and Portmeirion Pottery from 1961.*

Talisman – *the pattern was initially available in three handpainted colourways or black on white. Most items are in the later format with printed background colour. Portmeirion Ware and Portmeirion Pottery 1962.*

Greek Key – *early tea and coffee items, Cylinder and Meridian shape (covered sugar). Portmeirion Pottery from 1963.*

Birds *(open-stock),* **Dolphin** *and* **Shells** – *bathroom sets, popular export items for America. Portmeirion Pottery c1965.*

Totem – *larger serving items including the punch or soup tureen. Portmeirion Pottery from 1963.*

Promotional leaflets.

Totem – *blue, ochre, celadon, white, ice blue and olive green glaze colours. Portmeirion Pottery from 1963.*

Cypher – *mustard, pewter, white, ice blue and brown glaze colours. Portmeirion Pottery from 1964.*

Jupiter – green and purple trial pieces, early blue glaze on teapot. Brown glaze and dinnerware items also available. Portmeirion Pottery from 1964.

Samarkand – *selection of colourways available. Lemonade beaker and ice jug on right. Portmeirion Pottery from 1964.*

Tivoli - *Serif shape, the transfer sheets for this pattern could be cut to fit different shapes. Bright colours were trialed but only green/blue and blue/brown were produced commercially. Portmeirion Pottery from 1964.*

Variations – *transfer pattern that could be cut to fit differently shaped items. Mainly found on Serif shape tea and dinnerware, the herb jar in pink and tan is a trial colourway. Portmeirion Pottery 1964.*

Monte Sol – *Serif shape coffee and teapot. Blue/green and lilac/turquoise were the colourways produced from 1965. Trial colour plates in foreground. Cylinder coffee pot, plate and mug are in later Marrakesh pattern c1968. Pink store jar marketed from the same period.*

Magic City – *this Serif shape pattern was extremely popular from its launch in 1966. Made on a wide variety of shapes including the mixing bowl and rolling pin and herb and store jars. A blue and green version was also made in smaller quantities. Portmeirion Pottery from 1966.*

Opposite, promotional leaflets.

Magic Garden – *follow-on pattern to the successful* **Magic City**. *A range of Cylinder-shaped tea and dinnerware was produced. Portmeirion Pottery 1970.*

Corsets – *on Cylinder, Serif and fancy shapes. A collection of images from Victorian advertisements made up this set, Susan designed the plate motif (right). Portmeirion Pottery from 1965.*

Chemist Prints – *originally referred to as Medicine Prints, these copper-plate images were rescued from Kirkham Pottery's attic. These advertising images were used into the late 1970s. Portmeirion Pottery from 1962.*

Left, **Reddington's New Foot Soldiers** – *toy theatre print available on black and white or two-tone background and later on plain, coloured glazed backgrounds. Portmeirion Pottery from 1966.*
Above, Designs taken from the copper-plate collection in Kirkham's attic. Shapes include inhaler decorated with Circassian beauty and a leech jar with the Shipwright's Arms. Portmeirion Pottery from 1962.

Favorite [sic] Horseman – *illustrations taken from nineteenth-century Pollock's Toy Theatres and 'penny plain tuppence coloured' prints. The jug in the centre is the large beach jug intended for tea, and the jug on the far right is a miniature, height 1ins (2.5cms). Portmeirion Pottery from 1966.*

Pantomime Characters – *toy theatre illustrations. This pattern featured in the 1960s television programme, 'The Prisoner'. Portmeirion Pottery from 1966.*

Country Life and Sporting Scenes – *these images, after Bewick, were used by both Gray's and Kirkham's in the 1950s. Portmeirion Pottery from 1963.*

British Herald *and Black* **Dolphin** *– Serif-shaped teapot and orange glaze, colour items. Miniature jugs in foreground and Cylinder coffee pot and store jar in* **Dolphin** *pattern. Portmeirion Pottery from 1966.*

Top, **Sailing Ships** *– produced throughout the Gray's period until late 1970s, these images were found on a wide variety of shapes. Generally found as black prints on white, on dinner, tea and fancyware, on Serif and Cylinder shapes including the rare miniature bedpan with compass motif. The turquoise glaze was used in the late 1960s and early 1970s. Portmeirion Pottery from 1963.*

Second row, from left, **Shakespeare** *– the 300th anniversary, glaze coloured and handpainted versions were produced including blue (not illustrated). Portmeirion Pottery 1964; trial shapes including* **Volterra** *in lime, black and white. The cup sat on the spike in the saucer. Portmeirion Pottery 1965.*

Above, **Balloons** *and* **Blue Holland** *– open-stock transfers used on Cylinder shapes. Portmeirion Pottery from 1963.*

Gold Six – *from left, Gold Sign (Serif milk jug), Gold Rule (Serif coffee pot), Gold Check (Serif beaker), Gold Flame (Serif coffee pot), Gold Section (Cylinder coffee cup), Gold Signal (Serif coffee pot and cup) Gold Section (Drum tea/coffee pot), Gold Rule (Serif sugar bowl). Portmeirion Pottery from 1965.*

Gold Brocade – *from left,* **Aztec Brocade, Coptic Brocade, Arabian Brocade, Persian Brocade.** *Portmeirion Pottery c1968.*

Cylinder coffee pots in **Royal Palm** *and* **Queen of Carthage**. *Meridian teaware in* **Gold Medallion**. *Portmeirion Pottery from 1970.*

Velocipedes – *selection of patterns on a number of shapes including a bottle and chamber pot. Portmeirion Pottery from 1968.*

John Cuffley, Susan's assistant in the late 1960s, designed the successful **Zodiac** *series (left) produced in various glaze colours and shapes and the long-running coffee set pattern,* **Phoenix.** *Other commemorative and limited edition patterns are for the Endeavour, the Apollo moon landing and the Mayflower.*

A Year to Remember – *limited edition tankards, airtight jars and smaller Imperial Tankards were also produced. Portmeirion Pottery from 1970.*

Trial designs including, Sacred Edifice, Lucky Fish, Paradise Birds, Disaster/Volcano. Front dishes, early **Zodiac** *trials. Portmeirion Pottery 1960s.*

Interior of The Ship Shop, Portmeirion village, c1966.

rustic scenes, decorative details and potential border patterns were among the contents and it took a great deal of time to unwrap and categorise them. Some of the rustic details were applied to tankards, jars and teaware in the style of the *Bewick* patterns and were decorated with the *Totem* glazes. These were probably not commercially available though some examples may appear on the open market.

Gold Six

After the success of the abstract patterns *Tivoli* and *Variations*, Susan produced her most daring coffee set designs on the Serif shape, *Gold Six*. Once again, she favoured the idea of a mix and match pattern with six designs all in the same palette of brown, black and gold on a glossy white glaze. Cut-out paper shapes formed the idea of the designs, giving a hands-on or hand-crafted look. *Gold Check* is comprised of small diamonds, squares and circles while *Gold Sign* is a more 'painterly' design with mystical symbols in black against medallions of brown and gold. *Gold Rule, Signal* and *Section* are bolder geometric patterns which Susan laid out on graph paper. These patterns are upright on the coffee pots and a reduced, simpler version is placed sideways on other hollow items, rather than using one large pattern on differently sized pieces. *Gold Flame* is the last of the set and the most

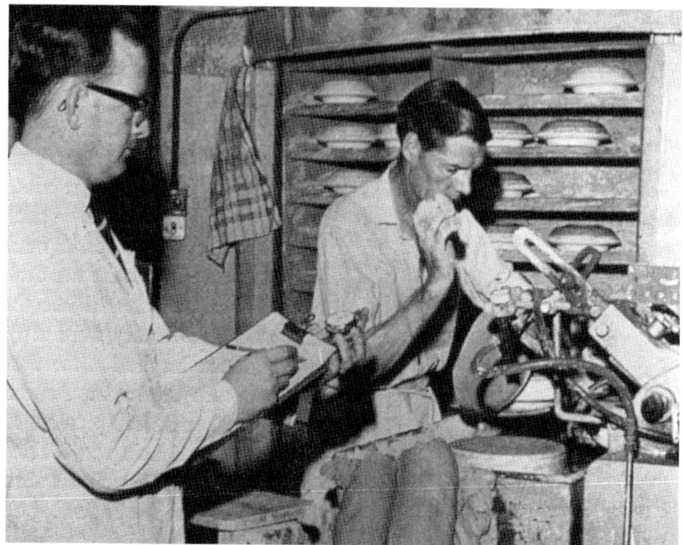

Plates in production, Portmeirion factory, 1960s.

Packing finished ware, Portmeirion factory, 1960s.

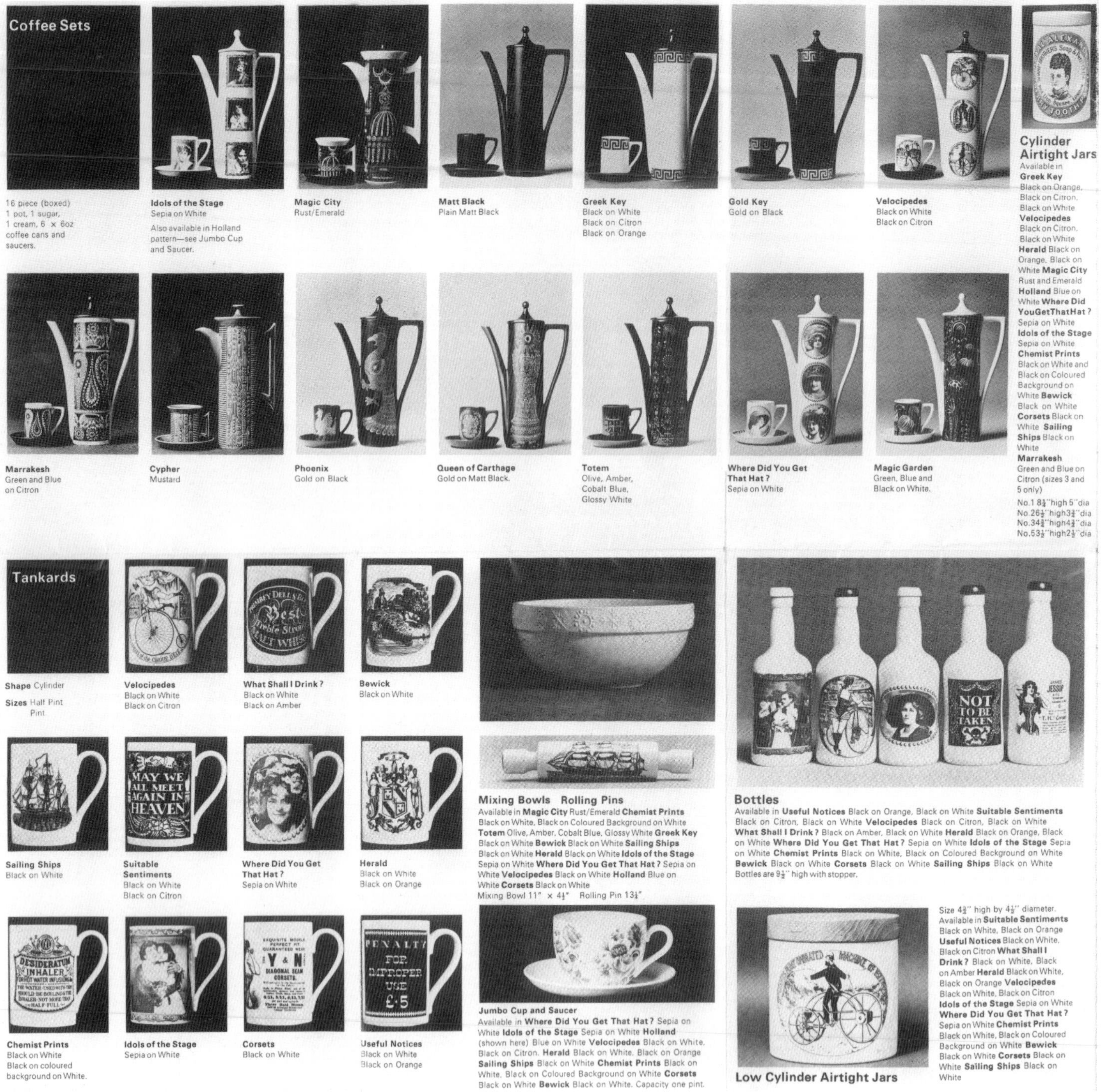

Coffee Sets

16 piece (boxed) 1 pot, 1 sugar, 1 cream, 6 × 6oz coffee cans and saucers.

Idols of the Stage Sepia on White
Also available in Holland pattern—see Jumbo Cup and Saucer.

Magic City Rust/Emerald

Matt Black Plain Matt Black

Greek Key Black on White, Black on Citron, Black on Orange

Gold Key Gold on Black

Velocipedes Black on White, Black on Citron

Marrakesh Green and Blue on Citron

Cypher Mustard

Phoenix Gold on Black

Queen of Carthage Gold on Matt Black.

Totem Olive, Amber, Cobalt Blue, Glossy White

Where Did You Get That Hat? Sepia on White

Magic Garden Green, Blue and Black on White.

Cylinder Airtight Jars
Available in **Greek Key** Black on Orange, Black on Citron, Black on White **Velocipedes** Black on Citron, Black on White **Herald** Black on Orange, Black on White **Magic City** Rust and Emerald **Holland** Blue on White **Where Did YouGetThatHat?** Sepia on White **Idols of the Stage** Sepia on White **Chemist Prints** Black on White and Black on Coloured Background on White **Bewick** Black on White **Corsets** Black on White **Sailing Ships** Black on White **Marrakesh** Green and Blue on Citron (sizes 3 and 5 only)
No.1 8¼" high 5" dia
No.2 6½" high 3¾" dia
No.3 4¾" high 4¾" dia
No.5 3½" high 2½" dia

Tankards

Shape Cylinder
Sizes Half Pint, Pint

Velocipedes Black on White, Black on Citron

What Shall I Drink? Black on White, Black on Amber

Bewick Black on White

Sailing Ships Black on White

Suitable Sentiments Black on White, Black on Citron

Where Did You Get That Hat? Sepia on White

Herald Black on White, Black on Orange

Chemist Prints Black on White, Black on coloured background on White.

Idols of the Stage Sepia on White

Corsets Black on White

Useful Notices Black on White, Black on Orange

Mixing Bowls Rolling Pins
Available in **Magic City** Rust/Emerald **Chemist Prints** Black on White, Black on Coloured Background on White **Totem** Olive, Amber, Cobalt Blue, Glossy White **Greek Key** Black on White **Bewick** Black on White **Sailing Ships** Black on White **Herald** Black on White **Idols of the Stage** Sepia on White **Where Did You Get That Hat?** Sepia on White **Velocipedes** Black on White **Holland** Blue on White **Corsets** Black on White
Mixing Bowl 11" × 4½" Rolling Pin 13¼"

Bottles
Available in **Useful Notices** Black on Orange, Black on White **Suitable Sentiments** Black on Citron, Black on White **Velocipedes** Black on Citron, Black on White **What Shall I Drink?** Black on Amber, Black on White **Herald** Black on Orange, Black on White **Where Did You Get That Hat?** Sepia on White **Idols of the Stage** Sepia on White **Chemist Prints** Black on White, Black on Coloured Background on White **Bewick** Black on White **Corsets** Black on White **Sailing Ships** Black on White
Bottles are 9½" high with stopper.

Jumbo Cup and Saucer
Available in **Where Did You Get That Hat?** Sepia on White **Idols of the Stage** Sepia on White **Holland** (shown here) Blue on White **Velocipedes** Black on White, Black on Citron. **Herald** Black on White, Black on Orange **Sailing Ships** Black on White **Chemist Prints** Black on White, Black on Coloured Background on White **Corsets** Black on White **Bewick** Black on White. Capacity one pint.

Low Cylinder Airtight Jars

Size 4¾" high by 4½" diameter. Available in **Suitable Sentiments** Black on White, Black on Orange **Useful Notices** Black on White, Black on Citron **What Shall I Drink?** Black on White, Black on Amber **Herald** Black on White, Black on Orange **Velocipedes** Black on White, Black on Citron **Idols of the Stage** Sepia on White **Where Did You Get That Hat?** Sepia on White **Chemist Prints** Black on White, Black on Coloured Background on White **Bewick** Black on White **Corsets** Black on White **Sailing Ships** Black on White

Promotional leaflet, 1970.

spectacular design with an abstracted comet image surrounded with gold thorns . Limited to coffee sets this pattern has become popular with collectors as it is so distinctive and redolent of the time. However, great care is required to maintain *Gold Six* items in good condition – the gold areas are easily damaged by overly enthusiastic cleaning and many of the items on the market have suffered and lost the impact they had when new. *Gold Six* coffee sets may be found in any combination of the six available patterns: most commonly with all items the same; some with, say, only the milk jug varying from its fellows; and the true harlequin where all six patterns are represented. Introduced in late 1965, the pattern was expensive to produce and as it did not prove as popular with buyers as other patterns of the day it was absent from Portmeirion's price lists by 1968. Although made for the Serif shape, remaining stocks of the transfers were used on Meridian coffee/tea services in the early seventies.

Magic City

Travel has always been a great source of inspiration for Susan, and past and present cultures have made their impact on her work. This sense of adventure and excitement is best captured in the pattern *Magic City*. Dome-topped buildings and fireworks peer out of a night sky in a celebratory fashion. Described on the

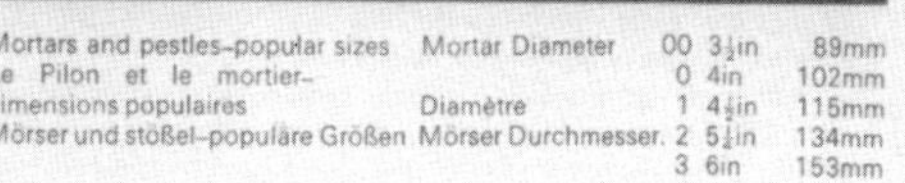

Mortars and pestles–popular sizes Le Pilon et le mortier–dimensions populaires Mörser und stößel–populäre Größen	Mortar Diameter Diamètre Mörser Durchmesser.			
		00	3½in	89mm
		0	4in	102mm
		1	4½in	115mm
		2	5¼in	134mm
		3	6in	153mm
		4	6½in	166mm

All designs by Susan Williams-Ellis
Toute la poterie est créée par Susan Williams-Ellis
Alle Entwürfe von Susan Williams-Ellis

PORTMEIRION

Portmeirion Potteries Limited
4 Portland Road, Holland Park Avenue, London W11
and Stoke on Trent, Staffs, England

PORTMEIRION
INTHEKITCHEN

Promotional leaflet, late 1960s.

promotional leaflet as rust and emerald, the black keyline is drawn in fine energetic lines and reversed, a technique Susan discovered with early photocopying where a negative image was produced. Blocks of rust, fawn and emerald were placed behind the drawing and the design came to life. Designed for the Serif shape with black accessories (lids and saucers), the coffee set was an instant success. This or the teaset was sometimes sold with six matt black teaplates although decorated versions were made as well. The pattern sold very well from its launch in about 1966 until the early 1970s. Dinnerware was well received, though the fragile Serif lids on the tureens are unlikely to have survived in great quantities. Kitchen jars, rolling pins and mixing bowls were being advertised in 1970 for the following year, but later production of the pattern is most likely to have been coffee sets only. Unusual items in this pattern include the set of six cork-stoppered herb jars in a wooden rack, probably made just before the change to flat wooden lids on Cylinder jars. *Magic City* was one of the first patterns to be sold through the major British auction houses in the nineties.

Gold Brocade

This set of four patterns again show the influences of early cultures and travel. Flamboyant shapes in different coloured lustres sit on a glossy black body on the hollow ware items, complemented by matt black saucers and lids. The pattern names give an extra sense of the exotic and historic, *Coptic Brocade, Persian Brocade, Aztec Brocade* and *Arabian Brocade*. Designed for coffee ware only, this pattern was trialed on matt white items but the gloss black gave an extra depth and sense of richness to the sets. This colourway became quite popular for interiors in the early seventies with ethnic metalwork and foil wallpapers, the developing techniques of screen printing making this effect cheaper to produce. The original designs were created by cutting the individual shapes in differently coloured metallic foils which were used as the artwork, so the finished design retained the energy and quirkiness of the hand-cut-out image. As with other patterns there was a mix and match feel to the sets – very often a set would have been sold with the cups in a different pattern to the pot. There was also an option to have tall beakers instead of the standard coffee cans. These patterns were unlikely to have been produced in large quantities and some have suffered in use with the lustres fading a little. A mint set is something to treasure.

'Open-stock' Transfers

Most pottery companies make use of what are known as 'open-stock' transfers, non-exclusive images made by manufacturers of transfers for use by any company. This explains why some images can turn up on a large variety of wares produced by completely unrelated factories. (Gray's and Kirkham's Pottery used these in their everyday output.) To increase their output, Portmeirion continued using selective transfers from suppliers, improving their productivity with cheaper, more mainstream designs than the expensive *Malachite* and *Moss Agate*. Some of these florals were interspersed with on-glaze banding in clean, bright colours or a line of gold to add a touch of quality. Others were used on wares for the American market but flowers seem to have been universally marketed and available in the price lists as *Assorted Florals*, one of the cheapest ranges. Rather than sell or destroy undecorated seconds, these inexpensive transfers added to output and could be sold with a basic decoration. When chamber pots were in constant

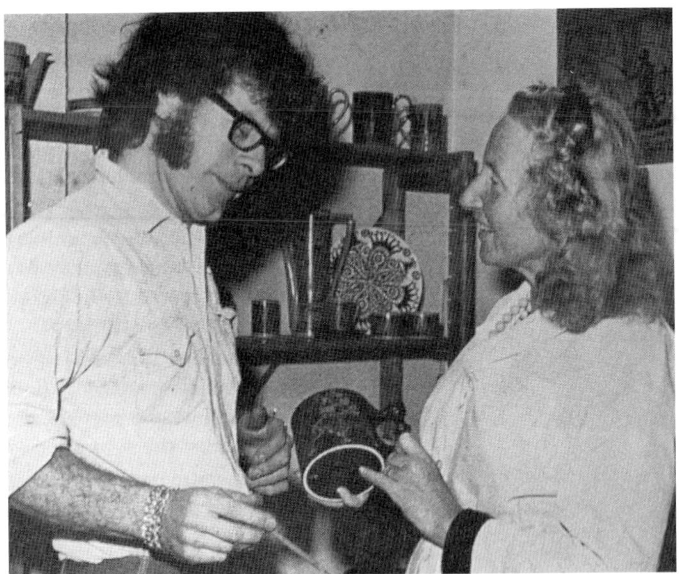

John Cuffley and Susan with **Apollo** *mug,* The Pottery Gazette *1969.*

'Libra' from the **Zodiac** *series.*

production in the seventies, many short-run transfers were used. Among the more exciting items with these transfers are 'glamour girls' and some historic balloons. Many seemingly enigmatic patterns can come from the open-stock stable.

John Cuffley

In 1967, Euan was spending most of his time at Blackies Publishers in London 'trying to make back the money the company was losing'. John Cuffley, a jazz drummer, had recently returned to Stoke from Hamburg, where he, like the Beatles before him, had been playing twelve-hour sessions in strip clubs and sleeping in cinemas between gigs. Cuffley needed work and had answered a newspaper advertisement placed by Susan. He was an unlikely candidate for a designer and when asked to show some of his work was only able to provide one picture of a house he had drawn for his young son. Nevertheless Susan took him on as, out of all the applicants he was the only one who had the 'look of an artist' with his side-burns and suede boots. Cuffley joined the company as Susan's assistant designer, using his calligraphy skills on his best-known designs *Zodiac* and *Phoenix* which sold well into the eighties. He also designed the best selling 1969 patterns for the moon landing and two commemoratives for the Mayflower's 350th anniversary. Cuffley took up residence in the flat above the old offices in Kirkham Street, which he soon turned into a typical 'hippy pad'. The rock and roll lifestyle never lost its appeal to him and in 1971 he left Portmeirion and returned to music, taking over as drummer for the Stafford-based Climax Blues Band.

Zodiac

The *Zodiac* series was a calculated risk as stockists were thought to be unlikely to want to order multiples of the twelve different patterns, but, as repeat orders flowed, Susan's confidence proved to be vindicated. Indeed sales of tankards looked set to exceed the best-selling coffee ware at the time. *Zodiac* was initially available on a range of shapes and colour options. Susan had discovered that it was not necessary to use the most expensive 'best gold' for use on matt black, the cheaper option looked just as good against the matt glaze. John Cuffley's beautifully detailed drawings were reproduced with a 'parchment' detailing the astrological background for each star sign written in mock 'Olde English' (a cunning mix from original texts). These were either printed on the reverse side of a mug or base of a plate, and after a short time the parchment outer detail was foregone in favour of larger text. Susan's notes indicate that she planned different colours for tankards inspired by birthstones or luck colours: Aries – pink, Gemini – cerulean, Leo – topaz/tourmaline, Cancer – jade green. The range was soon restricted to the best-selling items – plates, dishes, bottles and airtight jars were discontinued, as was the black on orange version. Imperial Tankards in black and white or gold on black, along with the half- and one-pint Cylinder tankards continued to be produced into the seventies. Limited productions with the gold image on a dark brown glaze, matt pink, purple or white mugs, and chamber pots bearing a single star sign are known. From a collector's point of view the gold on black sets (discontinued c1983), are the easiest sets to complete, though the alternative colourways would offer a challenge.

Phoenix

This design in Cuffley's highly original style is probably thought of as distinctly 'seventies' although it emerged in 1968 as the quintessential wedding gift for young homemakers. The pattern lived up to its name and was the last surviving Cylinder pattern in production, available on coffee sets until 1983. Printed in gold on matt black, each of the pieces has the same motif, reduced to fit each item. Although only produced on coffee sets the pattern does

Catherine Rooke's sketch for the Silver Jubilee design, 1977.

It was reported that many of Hugh's tankards were featured in the journal of the Commemorative Collectors Society. The semi-political mugs proved the most popular: Foulerton had received much publicity in 1974 when he made a mug to commemorate a by-election success by the Liberal Party. A few famous political names also collected his political mugs, among them Prime Ministers Edward Heath and James Callaghan. While a newspaper report from 1975 says that Hugh was already preparing for 1977 and the Queen's Silver Jubilee, an occasion guaranteed to sell thousands of mugs, no examples of his work have been found later than 1975.

Bottles

The Gin Bottle was an unusual gift item probably based on an original Kirkham shape inherited from the old factory by Portmeirion along with moulds for various miniature bottles. Various sepia and black and white designs were used to decorate gin bottles from 1968 to 1972, with *Sailing Ships* on blue or white being the most commonly found, but *Zodiac* and *National Trust Anniversary* bottles are worth looking out for. After a gap of six years the Gin Bottle was briefly re-introduced and from 1978 to 1983 almost all Portmeirion's contemporary motifs including *Botanic Garden, Birds of Britain, Orange and Lemons* and *Romantica* were available. Examples of bottles are generally scarce but one in particular will be very difficult to acquire: Portmeirion produced a matt black bottle for James Grant & Company for their Highland Park, forty-year-old single malt, unopened examples of which now sell to whisky experts for between £500 and £700.

Sepia Prints

As a natural progression from the black and white images on Portmeirion's pottery the new decade brought with it a new look. Susan had taken images from old engravings, advertisements and copper plates to achieve the stylish look of the sixties and looked to the photographs of the early part of the century for new inspiration. A sepia photograph had been turned into *Ermina Celli* in the *Velocipedes* series of designs and with more reliable printed transfers it seemed possible to reproduce these images to a standard suitable for pottery. The Edwardian sheet music for *Where did you get that Hat* inspired a pattern of the same name. Unlikely models of all ages sporting equally unlikely millinery were set into a border pattern of stylised pearls and printed in sepia. These were placed on plates, coffee sets and the still popular jumbo cups and saucers, the saucers with a border pattern and no central image while the cups had a smiling beauty set into an oval pearl frame. Launched in 1970 it seems likely that *Idols of the Stage* made its debut at the same time and was placed on much the same ware. Cylinder tankards were a popular item in the larger pint size and there seems to be a range of portraits of brooding actors and starstruck couples set in ornate frames; store jars with wooden stoppers featured Nordic-looking kings, and pensive actors. Much of the factory output of these items was exported to Scandinavia and Europe. Many of the *Idols* items have turned up in France with the 'Chaumette Paris' backstamp and no Portmeirion credit, whilst the coffee items seem to be elusive. Perhaps the images were too light hearted for serious dinner parties in the United Kingdom, but that was exactly what appealed to the Scandinavians as the designs became an after dinner talking point.

A cheeky range called *What the Butler Saw* was trialed extensively at this time (1970-72). Susan raided her collection of Edwardian postcards to obtain images of strong men and artistically posed female models in various stages of undress. These were collaged onto Susan's painted backgrounds to produce humorous scenes which Susan worked into with paint to heighten or add details. Coffee cans and teacups had quotes inside to add to the surreal and slightly risque pictures. A full selection of designs for flatware and teaware went into trial transfer stage but when the proofs were fired the original photographic images had scanned badly forming a 'moire' pattern and obscuring the finer details. The pattern went no further despite the interest of the Swedish store, Ikea. The backstamp featured a pair of glasses and 'Pop Art' lettering and is a great period piece in itself.

Designed for the American market, a sepia range of Victorian and Edwardian moustachioed gentlemen on shaving mugs, would have made a fitting complement to the women sporting oversized hats on other wares. It is not known whether or not these were marketed as no paperwork has yet come to light regarding the pattern. Along similar lines but abandoned before production, was a range of period views intended for mugs and dishes with scenes of London for which John Cuffley prepared the artwork in 1969. Susan's collection of images of Edwardian ladies cradling their dogs also reached the proof transfer stage and went no further.

What the Butler Saw *backstamp.*

Part Two

A New Era – The Botanic Garden Years

Old Staffordshire and Relief Ware

Soon after acquiring Kirkham's factory, Susan Williams-Ellis made a happy discovery. While rummaging in a long-disused attic she came across a soot-covered heap of roughly cylindrical objects barely identifiable under the dust and dirt of many decades. Susan brushed away at them and emerged triumphant, clasping the first of an important cache of over fifty Victorian jug moulds. A lengthy period of research and sorting followed. The moulds were bought by Kirkham's many years before in 1914, so there was now no indication which jug belonged with which handle. Susan scoured antique shops and museums, and consulted numerous books to identify the patterns and see how they were originally put together. By September 1961 Portmeirion was selling a variety of reproduction Victorian relief jugs under the Kirkham's brand of *Old Staffordshire*, a range that has gone through various incarnations and is produced today as *The British Heritage Collection*. Susan and Euan have their own collection of Victorian embossed jugs, initially to help in their research, but this expanded into a private museum with examples from all over the world.

Parian ware and other relief jugs became very popular in the period from 1830-1870 and are recognisable by their ornate shapes and embossed decoration. Aimed at the newly prosperous Victorian middle-class, the different sized jugs were used to serve hot and cold liquids, water, beer, toddy, milk or cream, at the tea or dinner table. Their introduction was the result of technical advances in mould making and body formulation, which made it possible to produce large numbers of jugs with high-quality modelling in fine stoneware and porcelain. The patterns varied from decorative to illustrative, some with biblical scenes, or popular songs or architectural styles, while others featured the Prince Consort, or marked International Exhibitions. The jugs, because of their social as well as practical role, are a reflection of the cultural background of mid-Victorian society and were an enormous success and produced by many factories. There were fifty-five Antique Embossed Staffordshire Jugs available from Portmeirion in 1968 including six sizes of *Apostles* (1 to 6), five *Beaded* (1 to 5), four *Cable*, one *Coral*, three *Dancing Cupids*, two *Distin Family*, one *Grape*, five *Hannibal*, one *Lion Tamer*, three *Naomi*, three *Nightingale*, two *Portland*, five *Pilgrim*, one *Queen Victoria*, four *Tulip*, three *Volunteer Rifles* and one *Washington*.

The jugs were available in white, brown or olive green glazes and are each marked with a generic Portmeirion rubber stamp. The same range included pairs of *Staffordshire Dogs* in four sizes, and hens in sizes Nos. 1 to 5 in white or brown (the size is on the base of the item)

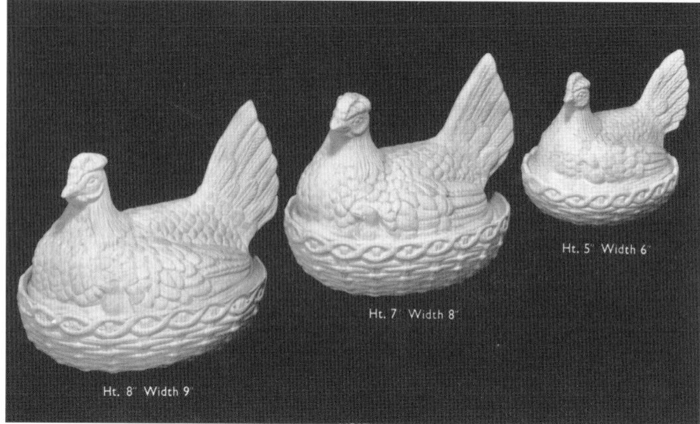

Kirkham's archive photograph 'Nesting Hens'.

Hens

It is clear that Kirkham's were producing traditional Staffordshire pieces under their 'Old Staffordshire' mark before Euan and Susan bought the company. Chicken-shaped egg holders have been a practical kitchen novelty for at least 200 years and have been manufactured all over the world. The introduction of the egg box and refrigerators with egg-holders has made the chickens more decorative than functional. Portmeirion egg-holders are instantly recognisable with the mother hen perched on a wickerwork nest, a chick looking out from under her protective wings. Advertisements from the late 1950s show the Kirkham chickens as white but the Rockingham brown glaze was also being used by 1963, and by 1968 Portmeirion had five sizes of chicken available from the largest size 1, down to size 5. By the 1970s the *Hens* were decorated in matt and gloss white and the three *Totem* glazes – green, blue and brown – and only available in three sizes. A limited number of miniature, novelty, single-egg chickens in colours including brown and blue were also made but are rarely found. Blue and olive green *Hens* were discontinued in 1973 (due to the relative unpopularity of these glaze colours) in preference for brown, the most commonly found hen colour. The small (No.3) and medium *Hens* (No.2) were withdrawn in 1983 leaving the *White Glossy Hen* No.1 to strut alone until its retirement in 1994. The variety of *Portmeirion Hens'* colours and size, and the rarity of colours such as green and blue make it popular with collectors of chickens. The chicken money bank made by Portmeirion as a trial and given to members of staff is a particularly prized item.

Duck

In 1975, Susan decided to add her own bird to Portmeirion's flock and the *Portmerion Duck* was launched in brown and white. Modelled and signed 'Susan Williams-Ellis 1975' beneath its tail, the mother duck sits on her nest (a No.1 Portmeirion oven-to-table chicken base) with two chicks beneath her wings. The *Portmeirion Duck* is Susan's only attempt at animal modelling for Portmeirion Pottery and the result has an elegant simplicity (1975-1983). Examples are relatively rare and the fact that they are signed by Susan may make their owners loathe to part with them.

Game Pie

In an age where blood sports are often frowned upon, the publicity for Portmeirion's 1972 *Game Pie* dish is unusual with the piece surrounded by dead game birds and a rabbit. Susan found the moulds for the dish in Kirkham's famous attic but decided that the handles – two knobs on the lid – were ugly. She took a cast of the ears of wheat on the sides of the base and used the relief motif to create two simple handles which it is hard to believe were not part of the original Victorian design. It was originally available in three sizes (Nos.1-3) in blue, brown, green and white but, like the chickens, the blue and green versions had disappeared by 1974 and the remaining colours were discontinued in 1977. This was partly because of the increasing unpopularity of game but more probably because of the crazing and staining which occurred when these items were actually used in the oven. *Blue Game* dishes are the most sought after by collectors because of their rarity and the popularity of cobalt blue. Green versions have never been seen by the authors but do appear in promotional literature; white is common but often found stained with meat juices, the brown-glazed dish remains the most commonly found in all sizes.

Dessert Plates

From 1975 to 1977, Portmeirion offered two sizes, $7^1/_2$ins (19cms) and $10^3/_4$ins, (27cms) of *Vine Leaf* embossed dessert plates in glossy brown or white with a pattern very similar to items of antique Wedgwood. Examples of these are unknown outside the factory – the number of similar items available from other companies, and the factory fires which occurred in 1977 may have proved fatal to this little-known and under-represented design. By the early 1970s Portmeirion had discontinued most of its *Staffordshire Jugs* but in 1975 decided to re-launch the *Grape Jug* in three sizes and two colours, brown and gloss white. Marked with a finer version of the old rubber stamp these are the most common older versions of Portmeirion's *Staffordshire Jugs*. It was not until 1984 that Portmeirion made another effort to market the classic designs in its archive.

Embossed Plant Pots

These were also produced in 1975 in brown and glossy white, featuring lilies, acanthus leaves and butterflies, a design which, maybe coincidentally, seemed to echo the themes of *Botanic Garden*. The bell or mortar-shaped planter has a recessed lip that suggests it was intended to take a lid, however, no lidded versions are recorded. Available in four sizes, $5^1/_2$ins (14cms), 7ins (18cms), $8^1/_4$ins (21cms) and 9ins (23cms) in diameter, the smallest size was discontinued in 1983 and the remaining three the following year.

Cable Jug Water Set

An antique design intended to appeal to the American market, the *Cable* water set was resurrected in 1977, the jug having been previously available in the early sixties. This commemorates the opening of the first successful Transatlantic Telegraph Cable in 1866. The body of the piece suggests the cable itself although the actual cable was far thinner. On each side of the spout are the American and British flags, while the base is adorned with telegraph tape carrying the first message transmitted beneath the Atlantic. The great showman, Phineas T. Barnum, is said to have offered a large sum to have the first message glorify his circus.

Antique examples of this fine series are extremely rare. To complement the jug, Susan designed a beaker echoing the cable design – six beakers and the jug formed the complete set. This was made with the gloss white glaze and sold as the *Cable Water Set*. Today complete examples of the set are rarely found and individual beakers are also hard to come by which indicates that only limited numbers were produced. The jug and beakers have an embossed 'Portmeirion Pottery Susan Williams-Ellis' mark on their base which is a feature unique to this version of *Cable*.

The British Heritage Collection

A major revival and the most successful outing for Portmeirion's antique jug collection began in 1984 with the launch of *The British Heritage Collection*. A new range of historic jugs was assembled which included some of those originally available in the sixties. A special technique was developed to reproduce the old Parian porcelain body in which some of the jugs were originally made, and to preserve the sharpness of the original fine modelling. Over the years Portmeirion's range of Parian Ware has undergone many changes but it still retains its popularity as giftware and among collectors. One change had to be made due to the authentic appearance of the range. In the early 1990s the original transfer backstamp was replaced by an embossed mark which reads 'PORTMEIRION PARIAN ENGLAND' to prevent unscrupulous antique dealers from removing the mark and selling Portmeirion items as Victorian originals.

Kirkham's archive photograph of Parian-style jugs.

Porcelain Jugs

The first items in the range were three sizes of the *Nightingale, Grape* and *Gothic* jugs introduced in 1984 and still available today. Later introductions included:

Pilgrim and *Cable* 1987

Miniature Porcelain Jugs:
Introduced in January 1985 this range of jugs, approximately $4\frac{1}{2}$ inches high, was separated into two collections in 1987:
Collection 1:

Grape 85-Present
Gothic 85-Present
The Huntsman 85-Present
Cupid 85-Present
The Tournament 85-Present

Collection 2:

Nightingale 86-Present
Hannibal 86-Present
George Washington 86-Present
Punch & Judy 1987-89
Mask & Flowers 1987-Present
Jewel 1987-89
Grape Harvesters 1990-Present
Babes in the Wood 1990-Present

Porcelain Vases
This series of petite bud vases was ideally suited as dressing table ornaments.
Arcadia 1988-Present
Water Babies 1988-Present
Hand with Flambeau 1988-95
Hand with Tulip 1988-Present
Rose Bouquet 1988-Present
Cornucopia 1988-Present
Pair of Boots 1989-Present

Porcelain Portland Vase

Surely the centrepiece of *The British Heritage Collection*, Portmeirion re-issued the 11-inch high replica of the ancient Roman Portland Vase. Better known in ceramic as the Jasperware version by pottery pioneer Josiah Wedgwood (1730-1795), this Parian Ware version of the cameo glass treasure was short-lived. Introduced in 1989 at £82.50 the price proved prohibitive. In 1991 the price was slashed to £50 to clear unsold stocks and the vase was discontinued in 1993. Examples of this vase, although illustrated on many items of contemporary sales literature, are very rare and the trial version of the *Portland Vase* lampbase even rarer.

Porcelain Figures

Only the *Swan* remains from this series of figurative pieces introduced in 1989. The rustic couples, *Shepherd and Shepherdess* and the male and female *Water Carriers* were designed as candle holders but were discontinued in 1995 though the *Shepherd and Shepherdess* were reprieved as they support the cornucopia on the *Arcadia* vase introduced in 1998.

Porcelain Plant Pots

Following the acquisition of the Sylvac factory in Longton, Susan had access to many of Sylvac's designs. The only one she considered suitable to re-appear under the Portmeirion name was a Romanesque vase depicting Neptune or Poseidon with dolphins, now known as the *Neptune* vase. The Sylvac originals are on a small pedestal, whereas Portmeirion's vases sit flat making them more stable for use as a planter. Launched in 1994 in three sizes, the *Neptune Planters* are still available. Other items not obviously grouped with the above categories are the *Rose* lampbase introduced in 1994 and a candlestick from the same year which was withdrawn in 1999. Portmeirion's *Parian/The British Heritage Collection* continues to evolve and the categories of the items change which, together with the occasional trials that appear, make this a fascinating field for the collector.

Meridian promotional postcard, c1971.

Mother's Day 1971

Although this commemorative only lasted for two consecutive years it was the idea which made the *Botanic Garden* series possible. Based on a handpainted design on a Staffordshire plate of 1815, the design was marketed along the lines of the *Year to Remember* series and intended primarily for the American market. Issued in 1971 as a numbered edition of 10,000, the plates were attractively boxed in a tasteful grey and white, with each plate numbered in gold on the back. The quality of reproduction was very good. The floral motif was litho-printed in colour with a rich, gold border pattern on the inner rim. The border was printed in pink, with self-coloured 'sprig-moulded' decoration of a mother bird protecting her young in the nest with symbolically outstretched wings. For 1972 a new floral image was found to fit the centre of the plate and rather boldly the edition was increased to 20,000 with updated packaging, but the design of the gift box was retained. The pattern did not go into a third year. The excellent quality of the transfers produced by a German company, giving rich colours and at the same time intricate detail, gave Susan the idea of using more detailed botanical drawings as a motif for tableware.

Chamber Pots

In 1972 Portmeirion was asked by its Swedish agents to produce chamber pots, primarily for flower arranging and as punch bowls. As Kirkham's, the factory had produced chamber pots for hospitals, but in nothing approaching the quantities it would produce as Portmeirion.

The first order was for 600 floral design pots for Sweden which resulted in a subsequent order for three times that number, and demand snowballed. At the peak, Portmeirion was making around 15,000 pots a week. In 1975, Sweden requested an additional item: the large pots were used as punch bowls so they asked for cup-sized pots from which to drink the punch. Thus the 'chamber cup' was invented. Numerous designs and lettering were put onto the chamber pots and there was a great demand for 'personal potties' commemorating 21st birthdays and wedding anniversaries. In 1975 the standard designs included open-stock flower prints and some black and white prints from the sixties including *Bewick, British Herald, Corsets, Sailing Ships, Velocipedes,* and standard messages such as 'Best Wishes' were also available to order. Retail prices were £2.30 for the large, £1.80 for the medium and £1.55 for the small pot. Special designs were individually priced.

Portmeirion also produced personal Portmeirion potties for many of the stars who visited Stoke in the seventies – in 1977 Tommy Cooper visited the factory and was photographed wearing his potty on his head! An enterprising shop owner in the Worcestershire village of Wyre Piddle commissioned Portmeirion to produce chamber pots bearing the village's unusual name and these proved to be extremely popular with tourists. It was proposed to celebrate the Silver Jubilee with a limited edition, large chamber pot decorated with a picture of the Queen and Prince Philip. Initially the Lord Chamberlain vetoed the plan but relented when an extra handle was added and the item was rechristened a 'planter'.

The only design not available was *Botanic Garden* which Susan thought unsuitable for a chamber pot. However, the basic pot shape was used to create more sophisticated

Kingdom of the Sea,
promotional photograph, c1972.

items: three sizes of 'Rose Bowl' with no handles appeared in 1976 exclusively in *Botanic Garden*, though these did not make it into the 1978 catalogue. Portmeirion introduced their last variation on the chamber pot theme in 1981 with three sizes of double-handed planters with horizontal handles similar to those of the old leech jars. Available in most designs these were discontinued in 1983 along with the standard chamber pots.

Meridian Shape

In 1971, after a meeting in Portmeirion pottery with Euan and Frank Thrower, who felt that a smaller mug was needed to fit current market trends, Susan had a lucky find in the local antique shop. She found a small Victorian cup with ridges around the body and applied designs in the centre. Frank thought it was just the right size and shape so Susan began to remodel the cup and developed the basic form for the Meridian shape. The ridges made the shape very strong so it was suitable for hotelware and the clay body used was called 'rockware'. As Susan modelled other items in the range it became clear that the shape did not need any decoration and, by having dual function items like a tea or coffee pot, the number of shapes could be kept to a minimum and save cupboard space in the kitchen. Interestingly no cruet was designed for the range – Cylinder cruet items were added to Meridian and Drum ranges from 1977. Speckled matt glaze colours were chosen to launch this new look in 1971: plover grey, saffron and terracotta were shown next to a deep mocha brown. Initial orders were good and it was a popular export range. However, the oxide speckles in the glaze caused problems in production so the three colours were withdrawn in 1973, while mocha lasted another year. A glossy white was introduced to fill the gap and patterns such as *Gold Medallion* were designed for the shape adding matt purple and white to the range of glaze colours. Black and white transfers left over from the sixties were used to decorate seconds and are very successful on the shape. Green and Rockingham brown versions were available in 1975 and 76 but the matt white was the longest surviving version, continuing until 1978 on dinner and teaware. Planters in the design outlived all the other shapes and were still on price lists in 1984. Until recently, the glossy white tableware has been in use in some of the self-service cottages at Portmeirion village.

Kingdom of the Sea

This design was described at its launch in 1972 as 'A series of ferocious fish for which Susan Williams-Ellis delved deep into the eighteenth century to discover'. These copper-engraved prints are reproduced in sepia on white earthenware to provide a similar effect to the original illustrations. Each is backstamped with the Latin and English names of the particular sea creature it bears and, in the same fashion as the early Portmeirion coffee sets where all the items had a different pattern, the plates show different varieties of sea life. There is an aggressive quality to the images, and they clearly reflect Susan's love of marine subjects. The range of exotic fish on 10ins (25.5cms) plates and oval dishes, crustacea on 8ins (20.5cms) plates and shells, 6ins (15cms) on plates and coffee/teaware, were taken from a French encyclopaedia on marine life. Some of the transfer images were even larger than those of the flowers in *Botanic Garden*, a few items of which were launched in the same year. Produced on the newly designed Drum shapes, *Kingdom of the Sea* was available as a 37-piece dinner service and 16-piece tea/coffee set with items ranging from 41p to £3.91p. Because the fish and crustacea transfers were so large, only the shell motifs were used to decorate the coffee/teaware and tureens, and these very appealing items are harder to find as are pieces in top condition. The earliest versions of the earthenware Drum shape are prone to crazing and stress cracking. Another problem was the use of individual backstamps to identify the items that have no identifying marks on the front. Unless the person applying the transfers has a passing knowledge of Latin or is familiar with fish species, they are unlikely to know which back stamp goes with which fish, should the pair be separated. This resulted in many incorrect fish/backstamp pairings and may be confusing to the collector. Multi-motif items such as the tureens, have the generic backstamp which shows Neptune riding the waves, pulled by dolphins. The misattribution of fish species on the *Kingdom* pattern was resolved with *Botanic* by the use of Latin and common names on the face of the item firmly connected on the same transfer. Despite its bold beauty, sales of *Kingdom of the Sea* were disappointing and it was discontinued in 1977. The design continues to attract collectors, including Anwyl Cooper-Willis who recently had the few remaining transfers made up into a dinner service. When Portmeirion launched its next fish design in 1981 it was limited to only a handful of motifs and was less adventurous than its predecessor.

Applying **Botanic Garden** *transfer, c1994.*

Botanic Garden

The Transfer

For some years Susan had mulled over the idea for a full colour design. In 1970 her assistant Kami Farhardi (currently Portmeirion's chief executive) was visited by a representative of the German printers, FX Leipold, who offered to proof some of Susan's designs. These were returned some weeks later and she was delighted by the excellent quality of the company's work – the original colours and brushwork had been reproduced perfectly. Previously, Susan had deliberately avoided natural colours and fine drawings, simplifying her designs so that they could be reproduced using the limited technology available to British transfer printers. Susan was so impressed with the results that she commissioned FX Leipold to produce the *1971 Mother's Day* plate, her first experiment in reproduction of high-quality antique floral motifs.

The Shape

The Meridian shape, intended as *Totem*'s successor, proved technically difficult. The random, speckled glaze showed too much variation between batches and had to be replaced by solid colours such as gloss white and Rockingham brown. Glossy white Meridian could be decorated with a variety of old and new transfers but the raised areas of double banding proved a barrier to uniform decoration. To provide wide cylindrical areas for decoration, Susan removed all ridges except the top one on the Meridian tea/coffee pot and cups and this new range was named the Drum shape. It was intended to be a compact range of dual purpose coffee/teaware, for example the cups without their saucers could also be used as mugs.

The Motifs

In 1971, while looking for eighteenth-century line engravings of sea creatures for *Kingdom of the Sea,* Susan and Euan found a brightly hand-coloured herbal book of 1817 in Weldon & Wesley, antiquarian natural history book sellers in London. *The Universal, or Botanical, Medical and Agricultural Dictionary* by Thomas Green (also known as *Green's Herbal* or *The Universal*), was illustrated with a wide selection of plants and flowers. The *African Daisy* with its vivid yellow and orange flower caught Susan's eye and this design was to become the centrepiece of the first *Botanic Garden Collection.* As Susan looked through the book she found other square-shaped, brightly-coloured flower prints that would make excellent pottery motifs. The square format meant that images did not need to be cropped as would have been the case if they had been portrait-shaped. Susan decided that rather than use a single image as a motif for dinnerware (as had been the practice for many years), she would find sufficient antique prints so that each plate, cup and bowl would be different.

The effect Susan wished to achieve was similar to that of the early nineteenth-century dinner services produced by companies such as Chelsea and Derby, where each piece of a service was skilfully handpainted with a different motif. She was soon touring London's antiquarian book shops looking for more illustrations for her project and her next find, *The Moral of Flowers,* was to provide eight flowers for the new pattern. The book is a collection of Mrs Hey's poems, prose and verse with literary and moral commentaries on forty-eight different plants from oak trees to daisies. The instructive text is illustrated with twenty-four delicately engraved, coloured plates copied from original drawings by artist and draughtsman, William Clarke, who had previously worked for the Horticultural Society (now the Royal Horticultural Society). Susan's copy of the book was inscribed 'To Julia', 24th February 1835: at that time, an interest in botany was considered a suitable and attractive interest for young women, and many lavishly illustrated books were produced with intricate copper engravings, hand-coloured to match the artist's original.

As Susan collected her material she considered how she could present the floral images as a design. She realised that something was needed to balance the colours and compositions of the floral motifs and decided on butterflies, moths and other colourful insects chosen from a variety of antique sources which she admits are usually unrelated to their floral companions and despite their aesthetic symbiosis may never have been found together in nature. As the design work proceeded, it was suggested that a uniform border would make the range into a cohesive set. Susan found a small, triple-leaf form, which, when repeated end-to-end formed a fitting border pattern. This was the now-famous *Botanic Garden* border, part of the Company logo and used on all Portmeirion's products. The name *Botanic Garden* was chosen to describe a mixture of plants and butterflies from many different climates, and Susan would also be free to add whatever flowers or butterflies she might wish in the future. *The Botanic Garden* is also the title of a long poem by Erasmus Darwin who was Charles Darwin's grandfather. Erasmus was a successful physician and spent much of his time writing poetry about scientific and technical subjects, including *The Loves of the Plants* and *The Botanic Garden,* based on a classical interpretation of the sciences.

By 1972 Susan had collected enough different motifs to decorate each of six cups, three sizes of plates, oatmeal bowls, two tureens, an oval serving platter and a milk jug. When the layout of a total of thirty-two motifs was decided, Susan and Euan went to Germany to meet the printers. The printers had never seen a design with such a variety of motifs and it took Susan three hours to demonstrate that all the motifs would fit on two transfer sheets as opposed to the seven sheets the Germans had originally thought necessary. The proofing process went smoothly and in 1972, the first transfer sheets for the coffee and teaware, bowls and smaller plates were ready for use. During this period the printing company had changed ownership resulting in a delay in production of the second transfer sheet, which included the motifs for the 10-inch plates, by a few months. As Susan was eager to market the pattern, *Botanic Garden* was initially launched in the spring of 1972 as a coffee set. The full *Botanic Garden* range of a 16-piece tea/coffee set and a 37-piece dinner service first appeared in the price lists in September 1972. *Botanic Garden* began a revolution in British tableware, soon dominating Portmeirion's output, and by 1975 it represented 43% of sales.

Susan and Euan continued to seek out new volumes to add to what became a valuable collection of antiquarian books. As she became familiar with the subject, Susan realised that the quality of some of the very first images, particularly those from *La Flora Des Dames* used on the oatmeal bowls, were not as good as later ones. Seeing the popularity of Clark's engravings amongst customers, Susan purchased more volumes with his illustrations, including Morris's *Flora Conspicua* and three volumes of *Medical Botany* by Stephenson and Churchill. From these came five further flowers including the *Peony* and the *Christmas Rose.* Portmeirion have not been able to discover much about William Clark, but believe that he may have died during the publication of *Medical Botany* which was issued in monthly parts – initially Clark's work was regularly featured, but there are none of his illustrations in the later sections. Portmeirion still works closely with the original German printers improving existing transfers in line with advances in printing technology, and developing new motifs and arrangements as *Botanic Garden* continues to evolve. After nearly thirty years *Botanic Garden* still represents over half of Portmeirion's turnover and is one of the world's most successful ceramic designs.

The Soup Tureen

In March 1982, Portmeirion launched one of its largest and best-known shapes, Susan Williams-Ellis' soup tureen and ladle. Originally produced as a display piece that would act as a focus for shop window displays, the design of the tureen owes much to the large leech jars Susan inherited when she took over Kirkham's business in 1961. Despite it not being intended for sale, orders started to come in for the tureen and it became a very fashionable wedding gift. Examples of the original display-tureens can still be seen, sometimes with added phrases such as PORTMEIRION STOCKIST in Portmeirion's familiar, bold Roman lettering. Susan still feels that it is probably one of the best shapes she has ever designed.

Portmeirion Stripe

In 1989 Portmeirion launched a range of fabrics and accessories in an attractive design with alternate bands of forget-me-not and rhododendrons running between

Promotional photograph of soup tureens, 1980s.

forget-me-not and rhododendrons running between parallel lines of the familiar *Botanic Garden* leaf border. Three background colours, black, white or red were available to coordinate with interiors. *Pomona* versions were also available in either white or *Blue Stripe*. The effect of the *Red and Black Botanic Stripe* is quite modern, resembling an Indian paisley print. The pattern was also used on wares and limited to an unusual set of glass store jars (Nos.1 to 3) in *Botanic Black Stripe*. Made in Italy by Cerve these short-lived, wooden-lidded jars are painted black on the inside with the design screen-printed outside. On the base in place of a backstamp, is a square black sticker with the lettering in white.

Variations

Using elements of the *Botanic Garden Rhododendron Stripe* design as a border and miniature versions of the *Botanic Garden* plate motifs, *Variations* on Botanic Garden, was launched in 1990 on the Drum shape, as a major re-styling of *Botanic Garden*. The motifs were arranged by Anwyl using her mother's *Botanic Garden* motifs and were available on a smaller range of items than *Botanic Garden*. The pattern was tremendously successful and sold over £2,000,000 in the first twelve months. The flower motifs in *Variations* have changed more slowly than those of *Botanic Garden*. The design was discontinued in 2000.

Botanic Variations

Confusingly, in 1998 as a special order, a limited number of *Botanic Garden* plates were made for Italy, including 6-inch plate motifs on 10-inch plates with a backstamp which reads *Botanic Variations*.

Botanic Garden Plate Mosaic

In 1995 Portmeirion introduced *Plate Mosaic*, Susan's motif based on coloured drawings of *Botanic Garden* plates. Originally destined as a fabric design, *Plate Mosaic* was used to decorate melamine and plastic accessories as well as oven mitts, but disappointing sales resulted in the pattern being withdrawn.

25th Anniversary Botanic Garden

1997 was a great year for Portmeirion. Susan Williams-Ellis' most famous pattern celebrated its 25th anniversary. By this time Portmeirion estimated that they had made around 25 million pieces of the now world-famous *Botanic Garden*. Susan felt that the anniversary should be celebrated with ceramic souvenirs and modelled two birthday plaques, one of a dresser with a birthday cake and one of a Canton vase with flowers, both to be produced in small numbers as they were to be very carefully handmade. (Unfortunately these, and another series of *Botanic Garden* plaques incorporating clocks never went into production, leaving only a few, mostly undecorated, trial pieces.) The *Botanic Garden* anniversary was launched at the International Gift Fair at Birmingham 1997, with a small collection of celebration pieces including: a miniature teaset sold in a satin-lined presentation box with its own tray and a book on the *Botanic Garden*; a silver-hinged one cup teapot; a sealed frame containing miniature pieces of *Botanic Garden* (known in the United States as a shadow box), using similar pieces to the teaset; a splendid jardiniere comprising a pot and stand with a total height of nineteen inches. Angharad Menna, also produced a limited edition print from a lovely watercolour, only 750 copies of which were printed, to be sold to collectors for £195 each. The most affordable essential item was a simple mug with the anniversary logo on the back.

Botanic Garden 25th Anniversary Book

The World of Botanic Garden 1972-1997 was published as a guide to the history, shapes and flowers in the *Botanic Garden* range and was included in the anniversary boxed sets as well as being sold through Portmeirion retailers. It is interesting to note that two versions of the book were produced, the original was sent out to members of the Collectors Club, and accidentally re-used the *Rhododendron* cup illustration with the text for the *Forget-Me-Not*.

25th Anniversary Party

In July 1997, Portmeirion invited all 600 of their employees, their relatives and friends, to Trentham Gardens, near Stoke, to celebrate the anniversary of *Botanic Garden* – with Susan Williams-Ellis and Euan Cooper-Willis as the guests of honour. The party continued through the warm summer evening with events from formal presentations to a varied programme of dancing including disco in which Susan and Euan put many younger members of Portmeirion's staff to shame. Money was raised for local charities partly by the directors of the company acting as waiters for their staff, passing their tips onto the collection box. Everyone attending the event was given a thank you goody-bag containing gifts, including specially commissioned *Botanic Garden* 25th Anniversary pens and enamelled badges now much sought after by collectors outside the company.

More Anniversary Items

As with the more recent *Millennium Collection*, Portmeirion found the demand for anniversary items was much larger than expected. So, in the autumn of 1997 they launched a further selection of items in satin-lined presentation boxes all of which included *The World of Botanic Garden* booklet. A jug and vase were decorated with non-standard *Clematis* and *Narcissus* motifs. A hand-gilded clock was also produced. Other more serviceable souvenirs included beakers, a pair of espresso cups, a teacup, saucer and side plate were also gift boxed and featured the Portmeirion's anniversary logo.

Botanic Garden *promotional leaflet, 1999.*

Wallpaper Borders

A brand new venture for Portmeirion in 1998 was the planned introduction of a range of eight different wallpaper borders, designed around the popular patterns of *Botanic Garden* and *Pomona*. The fifteen-foot, ready pasted borders came in three widths, narrow, medium and wide. *Botanic Garden* wallpaper was used to decorate the Hercules Restaurant in Portmeirion village in 1997 – the design was a diamond-shaped lattice of the green border leaves from *Botanic Garden* with butterflies resting in the centre of an occasional diamond. This and a wallpaper border depicting views of Portmeirion village were never officially launched in Britain and do not appear in Portmeirion's price list despite being promoted through the Collectors Club and other company literature.

Botanic Garden – Garden Range

Encouraged by their growing relationship with the chain Wyevale Garden Centres, Portmeirion made serious inroads into the world of gardening related items. *The Indoor Gardening Collection* as it was originally named when launched at the NEC Gift Fair in the autumn of 1997 appeared on the first page of the Portmeirion price list for 1998 under the heading 'Gardening Range in *Botanic Garden*'. The new pottery consisted of a three-pint watering can, eleven-inch cylindrical planter and four sizes of traditionally-shaped, frost-proof flower pots in heights

Botanic Garden *dinner-plate motifs, available 1999.*

of three to nine inches. A jardiniere had also been launched during the previous year to celebrate the anniversary of *Botanic Garden*. The ceramic collection was complemented by three textile items in a 'Botanic Gardener' print. In fresh shades of green, *Botanic Garden* pots, vases and planters are scattered across a heavy, unbleached canvas. The plastic-lined gardener's tote bag and apron both had pockets for carrying essentials such as the miniature fork and trowel set also supplied by Portmeirion. Although the ceramic items are still available in the main *Botanic Garden,* range the 'Botanic Gardener' textile items were discontinued in 1999.

Blue Garland

Starting life in working drawings as *Blue Wreath,* this pattern was a reworking of a nineteenth-century Scandinavian design. Re-interpreted by Susan in shades of blue and green, a simple band of leaves is interspersed with yellow-centred blue flowers. Early sketches show the pattern was intended for 'everyday quality' possibly as a cheaper alternative to *Botanic Garden*. Made for a large variety of shapes, Cylinder coffee sets were produced, dinnerware on a variety of shapes and also teaware on Drum- and Meridian-shaped wares. *Blue Garland* was listed in the pattern books until 1977 and probably withdrawn to make way for the major pattern *Birds of Britain* the following year.

Ballooning Animals - Nursery Design

Open-stock transfers of cartoon animals in the gondolas of gaily coloured, and even fish-shaped balloons were used for a short time on a giftware range. This nursery design was originally used in 1975 to decorate a small selection of Drum-shaped items. The range was intended for small children and included the small cup and saucer, beaker, six-inch and eight-inch plates and a gratin dish (ideal for use as a child's bowl). A small chamber pot was also decorated with the lively transfer. Officially withdrawn in 1978 this fantastical airborne menagerie, which includes a giant purple mouse holding a blue cat, an orange elephant and a purple giraffe, reappeared during Christmas 1998 when remaining stocks of the transfer were used to decorate seconds of the alphabet plate and loving cup shapes from the *Enchanted Garden* range.

Portmeirion Wales

In February 1973 Portmeirion announced that they had outgrown their existing Stoke premises and intended to build a new factory in the North Wales Tourist and Development Area at an estimated cost of over half a million pounds. A site was acquired in the town of Penrhyndeudraeth a mile to the east of Portmeirion village. Work on the 10 acre site was scheduled to begin in autumn 1973. The Pottery site was planned as a combination of a single-storey factory unit and tourist attraction in the style of the successful Hornsea Pottery Visitors Centre in Yorkshire. It was estimated that the project would be ready in early 1976 when the company planned to start production of a completely new ceramic product at the site. (The 200 factory workers in Stoke were assured that their would be no run down of any kind at their factory up to the end of 1976 but after that the company would decide whether to concentrate activities at one site.) Susan Williams-Ellis produced a rough airview of the proposed Penrhyn Site which included an ornamental lake, swimming pool, museum and terraced cafe. The entrance to the site was to be guarded by a cattle grid 'so we can have sheep instead of mowing machines'. However Susan's planned centre was never built. It was felt that the construction of a large factory complex in Wales was impractical as the ancillary services required by a major pottery were not locally available. Portmeirion's management decided instead that they would extend the existing Stoke factory by developing the land adjoining Penkhull New Road as part of an extensive three-stage expansion plan. A new loading bay and urgently required finishing warehouse was completed in October 1974, and many of the old factory buildings were demolished during the Summer Potters' Holiday to make way for a single-storey building to house production equipment and new kilns. Finally, the old Kirkham Street entrance was sealed off and it was planned to remove the old kilns from beneath the office block but, unfortunately, these were still in place in 1977 when they were the cause of a devastating fire. Portmeirion retained part of the Penrhyndeudraeth plot with the intention of building a small factory there some time in the future but it was not until 1978 that Portmeirion finally opened their Welsh factory.

In October 1978, 'The Crochendy', Penrhyndeudraeth's new pottery factory, was completed with the backing of the Development Board for Rural Wales and the factory was officially opened by the local Member of Parliament, Mr Dafydd Ellis Thomas. The 6,000 square-foot factory was expected to employ fifty staff within a couple of years but unfortunately the maximum number never exceeded fifteen. Supervising the workforce was Mrs Margaret Roberts of Gellilyden with Susan's son, Robin Llywelyn as Clay Manager. The staff was drawn from north west Merioneth and Penrhyn and was initially trained in Stoke. The firm had taken over a light and airy building first set up by the Development Board of Rural Wales in 1976. At the opening ceremony Mr Chris Madigan, managing director of Portmeirion Shops said, 'At the moment we have nine people working here but we shall be taking more on all the time'.

Since the days of The Ship Shop, Portmeirion Pottery had enjoyed a strong connection with Portmeirion village. By the seventies there were seven Portmeirion shops in North Wales - including two in the village, two in nearby Porthmadog and the Market Hall in Tremadog. A young paintress, Iona Hughes had been commissioned to decorate whiteware from Stoke at a small pottery in Llanfrothen for sale in Portmeiron's Welsh shops. In late 1978 she joined the staff at the Crochendy. Her designs were based on examples supplied on Portmeirion shapes by Susan Williams-Ellis' youngest daughter, Angharad Menna Cwper. Iona was the only hand-paintress producing floral and bird motifs in the style of traditional Llanelli ware, but most of her time was spent with the other four female decorators applying transfers. The main function of the new site was to supply decorated seconds for Portmeirion's Welsh shops. Whiteware seconds were shipped over from Stoke, transfers applied and fired in the factory's own small kiln before being sent out to the local shops. The site had a minimum staff with one man and two boys loading the kiln and packing the finished goods, and five female decorators all working under the manager Margaret Roberts. Prior to her appointment at the factory, Margaret had worked at Portmeirion village for many years as an assistant buyer for the various village shops. She recalls that getting services laid on to the new site was very troublesome and at one stage she had to use the public phone box in Penrhyndeudraeth to take orders. Plans to extend the factory were thwarted by the lack of a direct gas supply to the site and therefore industrial scale kilns could not be installed. The 'Crochendy' decorated seconds items with various transfers including: *Botanic Garden, Birds of Britain. Oranges and Lemons, Assorted Florals* and other inexpensive open-stock transfers. They also produced quantities of lettered items in both Welsh and English. So canisters with SIWGWR (sugar) in Portmeirion's bold typeface are still in use in many homes near Portmeirion village. The backstamp for the Welsh items was the red dragon of Wales and PORTHMEIRION CYNNYRCH CYMRU (Portmeirion Made in Wales). Handpainted items by Iona Hughes do not have a transfer backstamp, instead the artist's signature. When the Stoke factory had recovered from the fire in its decorating department and increased its capacity, it became hard to justify the expense of maintaining the Crochendy site. Whiteware seconds were being decorated so efficiently in Stoke that few were left to send to Wales and the vehicles that delivered first-quality items also began to bring decorated seconds. Following the production of two attractive 10-inch plate motifs commemorating the two major Eisteddfods of North and South Wales in 1982, Crochendy closed in the autumn and the building was used for warehousing. Stoke continued to supply both first- and second-quality goods to Portmeirion village and also supplied Meridian and Fluted whiteware for the Hotel and self-catering cottages.

Oranges and Lemons

Susan painted the original design while in Ibiza and, as one of the most lively and fresh patterns of the time, she and Euan decided to use it in their Ibiza home. Subtle details

The present façade of the Portmeirion factory, London Road, Stoke-on-Trent.

set this pattern apart from its rivals: the saucers are decorated with sprigs of foliage but when the cup is placed on the saucer, the leaves radiate from the edge of the cup. Small items such the salt and pepper pots are decorated with either the orange or lemon motif, and all larger pieces have a circular motif with a fruit-laden branch of each tree intertwined, the lemon branch has delicate white flowers among the fruits. A screen-printed design, this has adapted perfectly to reproduction and has lost nothing in translation. One of the most impressive items is the large Drum-shaped planter which shows to full effect the painted quality of the image. From its launch in 1975, the pattern proved popular, particularly in Wales. *Orange and Lemons* was one of the designs used extensively at Portmeirion's small Welsh factory to decorate seconds. It was withdrawn in 1983 but the design may yet reappear as, at the time of writing, it is being tried on new shapes .

Rose and Passion Flower

Unlike the harder almost technical botanical drawings on other patterns, *Rose and Passion Flower* has a softer look. The design is taken from a late eighteenth-century watercolour, and is a relaxed composition worked in blue, greens and pink. These are combined with a pale blue border of petal-shaped brushstrokes on flatware. Originally conceived as a giftware range and sold at the same price as *Botanic Garden* items, the collection was extended a month after first going on sale to include the same breadth of items as *Botanic Garden*. Appearing on price lists for 1978 but possibly available in late 1977, *Rose and Passion Flower* (along with other patterns) was discontinued in 1983 in a move to rationalise production.

Birds of Britain

Originally conceived in 1974, the illustrations for this range were taken from the book *Natural History of British Birds* by Edward Donovan, published in 1794. Once Susan and Euan had decided to use designs from Donovan's book they had to wait nine months for a complete copy to turn up at auction. It contained 240 beautifully coloured illustrations of the birds native to Britain in the eighteenth century. From these, Susan chose forty to use in the collection, *Birds of Britain*. This valuable book was then

General packaging artwork by Susan Williams-Ellis, 1980s.

sent to FX Leipold, the reproduction house in Germany. The original colours were so subtle and delicate that they were difficult to reproduce and the whole process took four years to complete. The lithographs were made by a Mr Bernt, the last design he worked on before retiring and so he 'put everything he had into reproducing the original illustrations perfectly'. His favourite bird in the collection was the *Gold Finch* or 'Distelfink', as Susan remembers he called it. The subtle illustrations were finished with a solid blue-grey band on flatware items. This helped unify the collection into a matching and cohesive set. Susan also produced a beautifully illustrated backstamp for the pattern printed in the same colour as the banded edge.

The *Birds of Britain* range was initially launched in 1977 as a John Lewis Partnership exclusive design in the United Kingdom, and in Italy for Bitossi and was generally available to all Portmeirion distributors in 1978. Although heralded as a possible successor to *Botanic Garden*, this design did not become as popular in Britain as it was in the United States and Europe. Susan thought this was bizarre as the British are famous for their love of birds. While the pattern was not fashionable in the sense of following a trend, this probably helped its longevity as it did not date and look old-fashioned. The *Barn Owl* was omitted from the collection to please the Italian and South American markets where owls are considered a bird of ill omen, a move which did not please customers from South Carolina where the owl is the most notable local bird (although the *Barn Owl* transfers are still occasionally found on seconds). The *Black Cock* was also removed from the range as its name was thought to discourage sales. These two patterns were replaced with the *Wood Duck* (previously found on oval plates) and a new design, the *Common Sandpiper*. Susan once said of this design:

> These birds refresh the spirit with the poetry of the natural world and reminds us of an age when man and nature still lived in harmony.

On each size of ware the birds were numbered from 1 to 6 for ease of identification. This method ceased following the retirement of the *Barn Owl* and *Black Cock*. Numbered transfers continued to be used well into the 1990s when stocks were eventually exhausted. (*The Compleat Angler* is the only design to retain numbered motifs as no designs have been dropped from the range.) A special machine that applied the painted bands to the clay had been bought to speed up the production process but resulted in faults that were not visible until the items had gone through the expensive production process. On wares where coloured banding could not be applied mechanically, blue-band transfers were produced but as each item required a specific transfer, this method was dropped in favour of the oak leaf border which could be cut to size on any item – before 1997, the oak leaf had only been used on the larger cookware items. Maintaining large stocks of undecorated banded and unbanded plates also caused a logistical nightmare in the factory. Where larger borders were required, a repeat motif of a tiny bird perched on a bough was used. Six small birds were used (smaller versions of the birds used on the coffee and teaware), which are not thought to be from the Donovan originals. After 1997 the banded versions of *Birds of Britain* and *Compleat Angler* (a later pattern) were discontinued but are available by special order until 2002.

In 1980 Portmeirion introduced a range of boxed *Collectors Wall Plates*'. Six each of the 10-inch and 8-inch plates in the pattern were sold with a hanging eye secured to the back of the plate with epoxy adhesive. In 1981 the 10-inch plate retailed at £5.35 and the 8-inch at £4.40 in contrast to the *Botanic Garden* 8-inch wall plate which retailed at £4.10. This reflected the fact that *Bird* items were generally sold at a higher price than *Botanic* (until all Drum shape designs were put on the same price scale in 1983). Although this price differential must have reflected higher production costs for *Birds of Britain*, it partly explains why this design failed to eclipse the success of *Botanic Garden*. The *Collectors Wall Plates* were discontinued in 1982 and some of the remaining packaging was used for the *Charles and Diana Royal Wedding Collectors*

Wall Plates, with references to their intended contents covered with a white label.

Strawberries

Portmeirion's colourful leaflet of 1976 first features Drum shape coffee and dinnerware in an attractive open-stock *Strawberry* design of leaves, blossom and bright red berries. This motif was obviously successful as, during the late seventies, Portmeirion's price lists mention *Assorted Florals* specifically including *Strawberries*. Concerns about the lead content in the bright red pigment of the *Strawberry* transfer caused major problems when Portmeirion's American customers asked Susan for a *Strawberry* pattern. An alternative motif was needed so Susan bought some strawberry plants for her garden in Wales. However, when summer came and they started to bear fruit, Susan's other commitments meant that she was unable to paint them herself. She then asked her daughter if she could paint them for the factory. At that time Angharad was studying botany at Bangor University and part of the course included botanical illustration. She spent many hours making detailed drawings of her mother's strawberry plants before painting the final motif of leaves, flowers and ripening fruit to be reproduced on transfers in a variety of sizes. Susan originally intended to call the pattern *Wild Strawberries* but this was changed to the more appetising *Summer Strawberries* for the launch in 1980. With the introduction of *Summer Strawberries* the older pattern disappeared from the United Kingdom price lists, but the two patterns continued to be produced side-by-side at least for export to Italy until 1983 when 'Old' *Strawberries* was discontinued. *Summer Strawberries* on a wide variety of drum-shaped dinnerware proved a popular summer design particularly with the Italian market but sales declined during the nineties and the design was retired in early 1999.

Fire!

At 4.45 on the evening of Sunday November 7th, 1977, decorating kiln fireman Len Picking was working with three of his colleagues when he discovered that part of the building adjacent to the old kilns was on fire. According to a press report at the time Len, who had worked in the factory since Kirkham's days, raised the alarm: 'I saw the fire at the rear of one of the kilns, I shouted to the others and while one phoned the brigade, we tried to put it out with extinguishers'. Unfortunately the country was in the grip of a fireman's strike and had to rely on the police and army with their famous Green Goddess fire engines to provide an emergency service. Two policeman soon arrived to help the kiln workers but were forced out by the flames. When more police and troops arrived they joined forces to control the flames which shot through the roof and shattered the windows of the one-hundred year old factory. The fire was prevented from reaching the rest of the building, the flames coming within feet of the sophisticated administrative computer equipment. Troops were on duty all night, spraying water on smouldering debris. Apart from water and smoke damage to transfer stocks, two kilns were badly damaged but, fortunately, parts of the building did not need to be demolished as originally feared. The fire had reduced the company's capacity but arrangements were made to decorate and fire some items off the premises. Production was soon back to normal. Sadly, Portmeirion's stock of black and white transfers were destroyed by the water used to douse the flames and the decision was made to remove those patterns from the price list.

The Compleat Angler

Susan Williams-Ellis said in 1994, 'People always say that you can't buy presents for men except a pair of socks or a Porsche', so she decided to introduce a range of pottery to fill the gap. What could have been better than 'fisherman's fish', an ideal gift for a man that 'wasn't too vulgar', could complement or inspire a hobby and would look as well in a study, a lodge or a country retreat. The pattern was based on original paintings taken from the book *The Compleat Angler - British Fishes* by M. J. Lydon, first published in 1879. Launched in 1980, as a small range it was available on a limited number of Drum shapes, mainly dinnerware and serving items. Typically, Susan found a wonderful image to use as a backstamp, dolphins and shells in Rococo style with the additional information, 'Fully vitrified oven ware'.

The fish motifs are seen at their best on the oval items although circular motifs in the range include more scenery and, originally, the same mechanically-applied blue banding used for *Birds of Britain*. However, like *Birds of Britain*, banding was gradually replaced with various sizes of the stock *Fern* motif in the mid-nineties. This transfer was previously used in its own right as a motif on Portmeirion's 1980s bathroom sets. Only seven fish make up the range, the original motifs in various sizes being numbered for ease of identification: 1-Salmon, 2-Great Lake Trout, 3-Sewen (Welsh Trout), 4-Gillaroo, 5-Alpine Char, 6-Perch and 7-Pike. The Pike is not as frequently seen as the other fish, being considered by some as too vicious a creature to be on a dinner plate.

Although never as successful as its counterparts (some retailers are reluctant to stock *it*, thinking it too male-orientated), sales of *Compleat Angler* have been steady since its introduction. As this design is still very much in production and the number of shapes decorated with this motif are always limited, most of the items produced in 1980 are still available at the time of writing, but collectors should look out for lesser-seen items such as the sugar shaker (discontinued in 1995) where the shape rather than the motif has been discontinued.

Pomona

Like *Botanic Garden, Pomona* is a subtle marriage of shape and design. Susan's basic Drum shape had its origins in the Cylinder shapes of the 1960s. By 1980 she felt that it was time to introduce a more rounded form. Taking her inspiration from a second-century Carthaginian cup she had seen in a museum in Ibiza, and the seedhead of an opium poppy, Susan developed her Romantic cup. Despite initial complaints that it was difficult to drink from, it soon became a particularly popular item and the basis for a whole new range of coffee and dinnerware in the Romantic shape. Even while she was collecting source material to expand the range of *Botanic Garden* motifs, Susan and Euan were also collecting books with illustrations of fruits that could have been useful as a sister motif if *Botanic Garden* were to become successful. The Romantic shape was launched in 1982 as the body for their new fruit design. The designs for *Pomona* – Goddess of Fruit – were selected from engravings found in copies of the *English Pomological Magazine* from the early 1800s, such as *Mrs Withers' Pomological Magazine* of 1828. The original, hand-coloured engravings were, again, magnificently reproduced by Portmeirion's German printers FX Leipold. Other companies have since attempted to use the same source material but have never been able to achieve the same intricacy and depth of colour found on Portmeirion's transfers.

First promotional leaflet for **Pomona**, *1982.*

As the number of items available in the Romantic shape have increased, many have been adopted into the *Botanic Garden* range, in some cases replacing the original Drum shape. As with *Botanic Garden*, changes have been made to *Pomona* since its launch in 1982. *The Red Currant* was originally *The White Dutch Currant* and the range also included *The Hazelnut* and two *Gooseberries*. Although no longer used on items as a featured design, the green gooseberry, 'Queen of Sheba', and red gooseberry, 'Wilmots Early Red', with names removed, are still used as a filler motif on butter-dish lids and on tureens, the gooseberries also supply *Pomona*'s leaf border. The largest design in the range is the extremely rare black grape motif *Raisin de Carmes* which was only available on the 15-inch oval serving dish and 12-inch bread crock, but is more common on accessories such as melamine chopping boards and textiles. In the autumn of 1994 two new motifs were added and the old plum and cherry motifs radically changed. The *L'Imperatrice Plum* was a print with which Portmeirion had never been totally happy, and a number of minor alterations had been made since its introduction. In its final format it had an airbrushed look which set it apart from the other fruits in the pattern. Improved technology enabled Portmeirion to produce the *Reine Claude,* a more luscious and richly-coloured plum. Collectors had commented that the *Biggareux* cherry looked unripe and inedible, accordingly Portmeirion altered the colour and made it into a black cherry, *The Late Duke*.

In 1998 Portmeirion introduced its large *Apple Trophy* motif which combines three varieties of apple: *White Astracan Apple, Scarlet Permain Apple* and *Red Ingestrie Apple*. This large circular motif decorated larger items, rather than having to use a larger version of an existing transfer or a number of small motifs. In the same year Portmeirion experimented with the *Pomona* motifs on a Portmeirion China body calling the design *The Fine Fruits Collection*. A short-lived Debenhams exclusive, this dainty tableware design was soon being marketed by Portmeirion as *Pomona China*. For the millennium, Portmeirion announced two new additions to the *Pomona* range. The *Princess of Orange Pear* and the *Roman Apricot* (originally announced for launch in 1998) replaced the *Teinton Squash Pear* and the *Red Currant* respectively. Each depiction, overseen by Susan, is in the style of original hand-coloured books of the 1830s. For many years *Pomona* was Portmeirion's best-selling pattern, after *Botanic Garden*. It was only with the introduction of totally new concepts in tableware designs such as the *Seasons Collection* that *Pomona*'s position might seriously be under threat but with *Botanic Garden* accounting for over 60% of Portmeirion's output in the year 2000, the number one spot appears unassailable.

Bathroom Range

Portmeirion Pottery released a new selection of patterns for use in the bathroom in 1981. This had been a popular

All shapes are by Susan Williams-Ellis unless otherwise stated

Kingdom of the Sea – *Meridian dinner and teaware featuring eighteenth-century engravings, Portmeirion Ware from 1972. The comport is a later trial.*

Where did you get that Hat? *and* **Idols of the Stage** *on a variety of Cylinder shape items and store jars, the coffee can (centre) and plate (far right) are from the* **What the Butler Saw** *series. The moustache cup and bottles were Giftware shapes. From 1970.*

Useful Notices *by John Cuffley –* **Suitable Sentiments** *and* **What Shall I Drink?** *by Susan Williams-Ellis. Portmeirion Pottery from 1967.*

Commemorative half-pint Imperial Tankards, Portmeirion Pottery 1970-82.

Lapidaire Alphabet *1968,* **Love and Friendship** *1972,* **Suitable Sentiments** *1968,* **Great Occasions** *1972.*

Ffestiniog and Talyllyn Railway souvenirs, c1970. **The Bottle** *1967, and recipe plate for Robert Carrier, c1970.*

Portmeirion Village souvenir mugs, 1969-99.

Football souvenirs – half-pint Imperial Tankards, 1970-82. Full-size and miniature replicas of the FA Cup, 1980.

Chamber pots, from 1972.

Limited edition **Mother's Day** *plates and presentation box from 1971 and 1972. The yellow and green versions are trials. Portmeirion Pottery 1971-2.*

Staffordshire – *Hens 1962-93, Duck 1975-83, Game Pie dish 1972-77, Antique Jugs and Dog 1962-68, Cable jug and beaker 1977-83, embossed plant pots 1975-84, Dolphin shaving mug 1962-85.*

Commissioned items for The National Trust 1970-1995; the cruet set, **White Almond Blossom** *for The Royal Horticultural Society, 1983.*

Plover Grey

Meridian
PORTMEIRION

Saffron

Meridian
PORTMEIRION

Terracotta

Meridian
PORTMEIRION

Deep Mocha Brown Glossy White

Meridian
PORTMEIRION

Promotional leaflets, 1971.

Meridian leaflet, 1971.

The logo from the first advertising leaflet of 1973.

PORTMEIRION

Front page from the first advertising leaflet for **Botanic Garden**, *1973.*

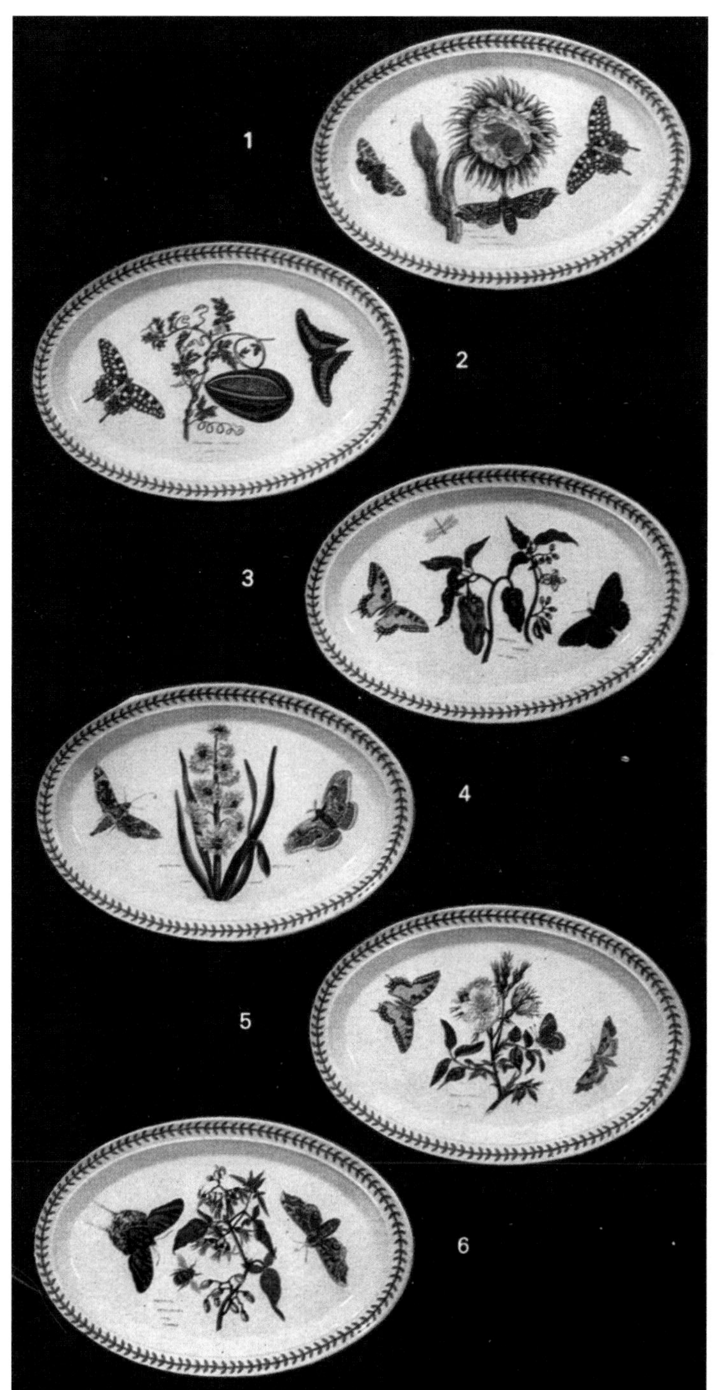

Promotional leaflet with the original complete range of **Botanic Garden** *tableware available in 1973.*

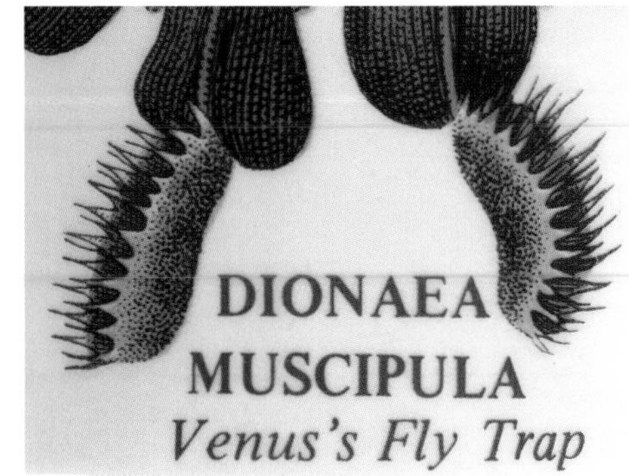

Printed lettering on **Botanic Garden** *motifs, 1970s, 1980s and 1990s.*

Botanic Garden – *(8-inch plate motifs) Woody Nightshade, Night Flowering Cereus, Red Peppers, Dog Rose, Water Melon, Oriental Hyacinth, 1973.*

Botanic Garden – *six-inch plate motifs, Bindweed, Aloe, Citron, 1972.*

Selection of original **Botanic Garden** *motifs, from 1973.*

Botanic Garden – *(oatmeal motifs) Cyclamen, Purple Iris, Canterbury Bells, from 1972.*

Botanic Garden – *six-inch plate motifs, Spanish Gum Cistus, Daisy, Meadow Saffron, 1972.*

Botanic Garden – *(10-inch plate motifs) Venus' Fly Trap, Passion Flower, African Daisy, Crown Imperial, Mexican Lily, 1973.*

Botanic Garden – *Honeysuckle versions, 1983 and 1994.*

Botanic Garden – *Convolvulus versions, 1972 and 1994.*

Botanic Garden – *(oatmeal motifs) bowl and plate Barbados Cotton Flower, Orange Cactus, Orchid, 1972.*

Botanic Garden – *early tureen motifs, 'Foxglove' and 'Strawberry Tree', from 1973.*

Ceramic lidded jars, c1980.

Botanic Garden – *Purple Rock Rose, 1980 and Treasure Flower, 1985.*

Botanic Garden – *Spring Gentian, 1972-85.*

Botanic Garden – *(teacup motifs) Rhododendron, Pimpernel, Heartsease, Tomentil vase, Speedwell, Forget-me-Not and Broom, c1972-85.*

Botanic Garden – *Austrian Lily, 1990-93.*

Botanic Garden – *development of double camellia: proof transfer, handpainted trial with notes by Susan Williams-Ellis on test tile, production tray, 1991-93.*

Promotional leaflet, c1980.

Promotional leaflet, c1979.

Promotional leaflet, c1982.

Promotional leaflet, c1982.

Promotional leaflet, c1978.

Promotional leaflet, c1982.

Promotional leaflet, c1982.

Above, promotional photograph, c1990.

Above right, **Birds of Britain** *– 10-inch plate motifs Black Cock and Barn Owl, 1978, withdrawn c1985.*

Right, promotional photograph, c1978.

Blue Garland, *1974.*

Rose and Passion Flower, *1978.*

'Old' **Strawberries**, *c1975-83.*

Oranges and Lemons, *1975.*

Double-handled rose bowls – **Botanic Garden, Silver Jubilee** *and* **Birds of Britain**, *1976-78.*

Compleat Angler – *promotional leaflet 1981.*

Book jackets designed by Susan Williams-Ellis, 1938, 1951 and 1983.

Welsh decorated items including Eisteddfod plate, 1978-82.

A selection of Portmeirion Publications.

Trade Union plates by Jack Stoddart – Tolpuddle Martyrs, 1984, and Peasants' Revolt, 1981.

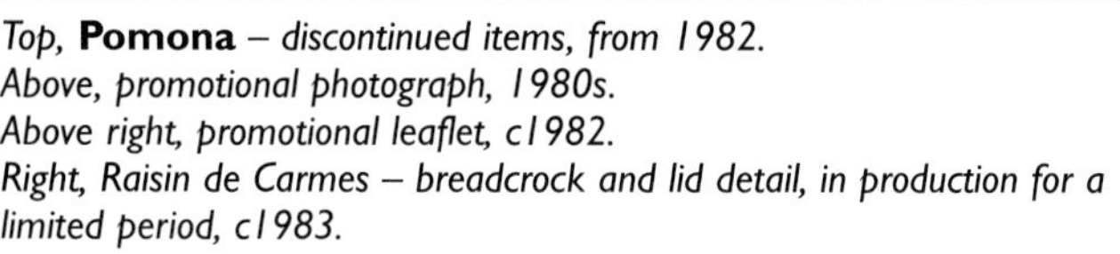

Top, ***Pomona*** *– discontinued items, from 1982.*
Above, promotional photograph, 1980s.
Above right, promotional leaflet, c1982.
Right, Raisin de Carmes – breadcrock and lid detail, in production for a limited period, c1983.

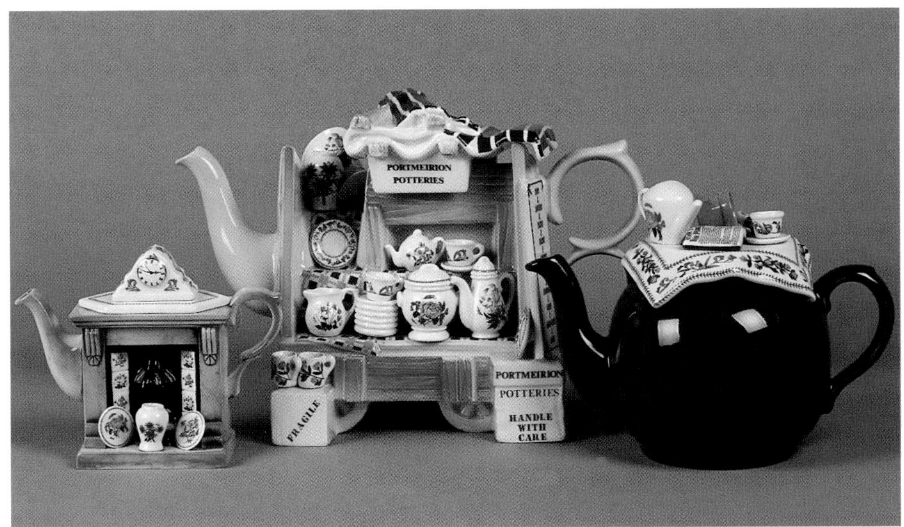

Cardew's Portmeirion teapots – Mini Fireside, China Stall, Green Betty (USA Exclusive), from 1993.

Botanic Garden *thimbles, 1985-86.*

Miniature hinged boxes, 1997-98.

Bone china miniature boxes, 1986-88.

Vases – Rectangular section, Ionic shape, 1984; Four Square shape, 1986; Cylindrical section, Serif shape, 1983; Hexagonal section, Manhattan shape, 1986.

Harvest Blue *by Angharad Menna – promotional photographs, 1995-99.*

Middle row, left, **Marble**, *1994.*
Middle row, right, promotional leaflet for a selection of patterns, Portmeirion China, 1994.

Left, **The Queen's Hidden Garden** *– promotional leaflet, 1994.*

Above, **Flowers of the Year** *(plates), 1985,* **Portmeirion Herb and Spice Garden,** *1998.*

Enchanted Garden *after* **In Fairyland** *by Richard Doyle, 1994-99.*

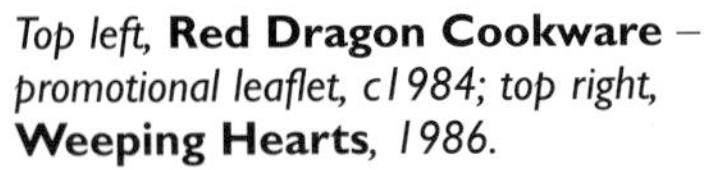

Top left, **Red Dragon Cookware** *– promotional leaflet, c1984; top right,* **Weeping Hearts***, 1986.*

Above, **Fluted White** *– promotional leaflet, c1987.*

Right, **Summer Strawberries** *by Angharad Menna, 1980.*

Spirit of Christmas, *1983.*

Below, bathroom china, 1982-85.
Left, **Countryside** *(open-stock transfer);*
right, **Botanic Garden***;*
bottom right, **Fern** *(open-stock transfer).*

Caption needed for pic 56

Handpainted designs 1994-1997

Top left, **Botanic Garden** *– plate, 1993. Clockwise from top right:* **Orchard Fruits**, **Barnyard** *by Debbie Wood,* **Dolphin** *by Debbie Wood,* **Sweet Pea** *by Angharad Menna,* **Aztec** *a trial by Julian Teed, and a leaf pattern trial designed by Angharad Menna.*

Handpainted designs

Top row, left, for Pugh Brothers LLanelli – 'Rhosyn Glâs' and 'Ceiliog Llanelly', 1993;
top row, right, handpainting in the Portmeirion studio.

Middle row, **Lemon Grove,** *1994;*
middle row, right, **Summer Fruits**, *1994;*
middle row, far right, **Kitchen Garden**, *1996.*

Right, **Mandarin**, *1994;*
far right, **Magnolia,** *1996.*

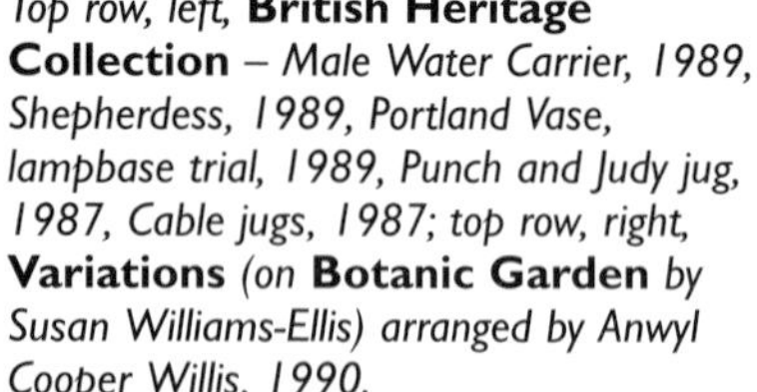

Top row, left, **British Heritage Collection** *– Male Water Carrier, 1989, Shepherdess, 1989, Portland Vase, lampbase trial, 1989, Punch and Judy jug, 1987, Cable jugs, 1987; top row, right,* **Variations** *(on* **Botanic Garden** *by Susan Williams-Ellis) arranged by Anwyl Cooper Willis, 1990.*

Middle row, left, **Welsh Dresser** *by Angharad Menna, 1992; middle row, right,* **Variations***, 1990.*

Right and far right, **Victorian Cooks Collection***, 1996.*

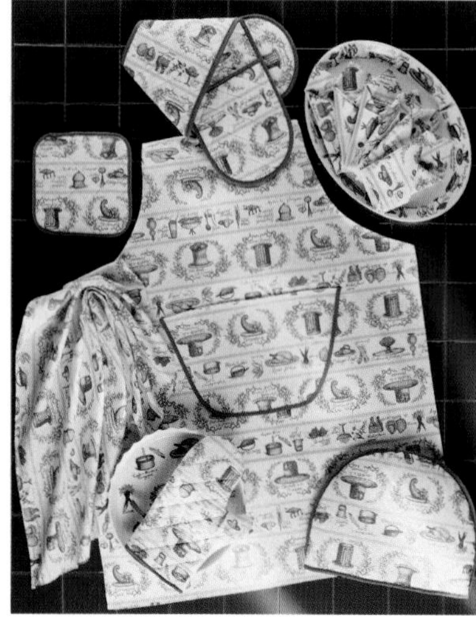

Botanic Garden – *oddities, Novelty Teapot trial, Ecclesfield Parish Church and Kew Garden special commissions.*

Botanic Garden – *25th Anniversary giftware.*

Second row, left, **Pomona** *and* **Botanic Garden** – *35th Anniversary plates;*
second row, right, **Botanic Garden** – *front and reverse view of 35th Anniversary Coral jug.*

Above, left, **Botanic Garden** – *25th Anniversary, Department Store Exclusive Collectors Plates;*
above, right, jardiniere for the 25th Anniversary in 1997.

Right, **Botanic Garden** – *Christmas ornaments, bells from 1992, plates from 1993.*

Millennium Rose *and Debenhams exclusive 13-inch Lily flowered azalea plate, 2000.*

Ñew **Botanic Garden** *shapes for 2000.*

Butterflies, *exclusive for the USA, for 2000.*

Seasons Flowers, *2000.*

Portmeirion 2000 – new patterns for a new millennium including rose designs by Susan Williams-Ellis and **Seasons Leaves, Dawn** *and* **Dusk**.

range of items in the 1960s and with adaptation and new decoration the range looked fresh and new. The range comprised a toothbrush holder, toothbrush beaker, a selection of store jars with a new domed, ceramic lid, a talc shaker and the re-introduction of the Victorian grotesque *Dolphin* shaving mug. A Victorian-style embossed tray was also introduced though existing examples are very unusual. In 1981 Portmeirion introduced gift packs of either single items or 2-piece sets. There were twelve patterns to choose from: *Botanic Garden, Birds of Britain, Summer Strawberries, Wild Briar* on a soft pink glaze, *Fern* (the motif that bordered *Compleat Angler*), *Bridesmaid, Water Lily* and *Rose* and *Passion Flower.* Four delicate floral transfers, exclusive to Portmeirion, and taken from James Andrews' *Language of Flowers* completed the range: *Water Lily, Carnation, Poppy* and *Pansy.* This range was discontinued in 1985 but the idea was revived in 1995 with *Botanic Garden* bathroom range which included a waste basket, lotion dispenser, pin tray and wall tiles.

Spirit of Christmas

This highly original pattern was produced for the American market in time for Christmas 1983. The heritage of patchwork quilts formed the idea for the design, from American Amish designs to naive 'Album' quilts from Baltimore, and one which Susan had worked on many years ago for her parent's house. All the designs are formed from cut-out paper shapes which took an age to complete, Susan even cut the tiny eyes for the angels and toys by hand, and plain and patterned papers helped to add to the patchwork effect. The pattern was launched at a time when there was a variety of exciting serving pieces in the Portmeirion repertoire. Three sizes of comport were decorated which could be stacked and used as one item. Vases, tea, coffee and serving items were decorated with festive motifs unified by the swagged greenery and fruits with red bows forming a border, and was ideal for a traditional, festive table setting. *Spirit of Christmas* made an impressive entry into the American department stores in 1983 but due to a marketing mishap the pattern was included in the January sales instead of being kept for the following Christmas. When a pattern had been reduced it was unlikely to be promoted again at its original retail price, so the pattern was sold to Sweden the following year and remaining transfer stocks destroyed, therefore examples are likely to be fairly difficult to find.

Red Dragon Cookware

This range of designer cookware was produced in 1984 on the new fluted shape. Intended to be both useful and ornamental, the range owed its distinctive glaze finish to the pieces being dipped in a black clay slip prior to the red glaze to give a *flambé* effect. The glaze settled in the recessed areas and the black 'undercoat' was more pronounced on the raised areas. This gave a slightly

Spirit of Christmas, *promotional leaflet, 1983.*

handcrafted and unpredictable finish making each item look individual. The promotional material described:

> The glowing red glaze derives richness of texture from the darker shading which also emphasises the shapes. It is a feature of this decoration that there is a degree of variation from piece to piece, to give life and interest to the pattern.

Although made to the highest standards the fully vitrified stoneware body was problematic in use and had to be withdrawn. The large lasagne dish would crack in the oven, and the glaze did not pass the stringent requirements of the United States. Items sold in the United Kingdom were withdrawn in 1986. Consequently, items in the *Red Dragon* range are virtually impossible to find.

Fluted Whiteware 1987-88

The *Red Dragon* shapes were not forgotten and they appeared again in 1987 on a range of coffee and teaware, with a matching range of dinner shapes and flan dishes. The cruet is particularly appealing in this range, resembling miniature Roman pillars.

Looses Cookware

In the mid-eighties Portmeirion produced a range of professional cookware including baking dishes, casseroles and ramekins for Looses Ltd., a chain of stores supplying catering equipment in Southern England. The items were fully vitrified stoneware with a simple unleaded glaze, available in pastel colours, based on the existing Drum shape.

Portmeirion Thimbles

The first thimble produced by Portmeirion was commissioned exclusively in 1985 by the Thimble Collectors Club and was included in a range of thimbles from various well-known Stoke potteries such as Wedgwood and Spode. Available in a Portmeirion Green pill box or in a printed envelope, the thimble featured the tiny purple and yellow flower of the *Heartsease* transfer with the base of the thimble edged in gold. It was reported in a flier from the Club the following year, that:

> Our members liked it so much that now the artists and bone china specialists at Portmeirion have produced a complete collection of twelve exquisitely beautiful thimbles especially for the club.

The offer was available only by subscription – thimbles were issued at a rate of two per month at just £6.45 each and subscribers received a polished mahogany display rack at no extra cost.

Each thimble featured a cut-down version of the following *Botanic Garden* transfers: *Common Tomentil, Scarlet Pimpernel, Rhododendron, Germander Speedwell, Spring Gentian, Star Anemone, Broom, Ivy Leafed Cyclamen, Daisy, Honeysuckle, Iris* and *Barbados Cotton Flower*. As the thimble was not a standard Portmeirion shape it is likely that china whiteware thimbles were supplied by the club for Portmeirion to decorate. The Surrey-based Thimble Collectors Club no longer exists and despite the regular appearance of *Heartsease* (the first), only a few examples of the 1986 set of twelve *Botanic Garden* thimbles are known to be in the hands of Portmeirion collectors.

Flowers of the Year

Much of Susan's other designs from this period were adapted images from antiquarian natural history books but *Flowers of the Year* introduced in 1985 was original work. Susan had developed the designs while planning a new garden. She had often toyed with the idea of making twelve small gardens, one for each month of the year, with flowers that would bloom in that month. She made sketches of some of the plants and these suggested her new decoration, *Flowers of the Year*, a sort of floral calendar of the English garden. The range included a set of 'Anniversary Cups' birthday gifts for each month of the year. *Flowers of the Year* was available on items from the entire Portmeirion range including Drum-shaped dinnerware. As with *The Queen's Hidden Garden* a colourful, fold-out brochure was made for *Flowers of the Year*, listing all the flowers and the wide range of shapes on which they were available. Unfortunately few retailers stocked the design and the majority of sales were made through Portmeirion's own shops where *Flowers of the Year* was available up to 1998.

January – Japonica
February – Jasmine
March – Narcissus
April – Anemone
May – Peony
June – Campanula
July – Rose
August – Carnation
September – Clematis
October – Fuchsia
November – Chrysanthemum
December – Christmas Rose

The Queen's Hidden Garden

This 1986 design by Shahrzad Forouzan (wife of Kami Farhadi) features:

> ...a rampage of weeds, or a botanic garden fit for a Queen. Take your pick, for a weed is a wild flower growing in a formal setting and all our garden flowers were once wild plants, 'weeds' whose virtues to be discovered.

The designs were taken from Marjorie Lyon's illustrations in *The Queen's Hidden Garden - Buckingham Palace's Treasure of Wild Plants* by David Bellamy. The famous botanist and environmentalist extols the virtues of 254 plants that grace the less formal aspects of Buckingham Palace and help to nurture no less than 350 types of butterflies and moths. The book was also available through Portmeirion Stockists to complement the tableware. The plants featured in the pattern are *Ox-eye Daisy, Pale and Rosebay Willow-Herb, White Red and Alsike Clover, Spear Thistle, Slender Hardhead, Coltsfoot, Heartsease, Meadow Buttercup, Lesser Bindweed, Burdock and Periwinkle, Winter Aconite, Columbine* and *Fratillary*. Unlike *Botanic Garden* the transfers do not include the name of the subject. Portmeirion's leaflet showing all the flowers, acts as a guide to the range, and includes the following message from David Bellamy:

> The food you will enjoy from these plates is brought to you by kind permission of the members of the Plant Kingdom.

Portmeirion Crystal

Taking her lead from the craftsmanship of Dartington Crystal, Susan Williams-Ellis designed a range comprising seventeen pieces including drinking glass, goblets and vases. Launched at the 1986 Birmingham Spring Show, each item had its own quirky name such as Pearly King and Flapper and came in a presentation box decorated with illustrations by Susan. The labels are a *tour de force* of her illustrative work. Portmeirion Crystal was 24% lead crystal glass and was limited originally to the United Kingdom.

Weeping Hearts

An eighteenth-century piece of Minton china was the source of this pattern featuring the flowering plant Bleeding Hearts. The pattern name was changed to the

Welsh Dresser
by Angharad Menna, 1992.

Promotional photograph, Portmeirion Crystal, 1986.

less morbid *Weeping Hearts*, and introduced in 1986 on a broad range of Romantic-shaped ware, but it did not enjoy the same success as other similar florals. Susan felt that the same image on all the items (unlike *Botanic Garden* or *Pomona* where the pieces or shapes have different motifs) lessened the design's collectability. The sweep of the flowers added a grace to the shapes it appeared on and the amazing breadth of colours in the leaves makes this a very striking pattern.

Welsh Dresser

Welsh Dresser by Angharad Menna, was Portmeirion's tribute to Llanelli Ware, one of the great traditions of British country pottery sold at rural fairs and markets for nearly 100 years. The traditional *Llanelli Ware* designs consisted of abstract and stylised floral motifs, which were swiftly painted with large brushes in bold calligraphic strokes conveying a tremendous vitality. Like many other folk arts of that era, in the early twentieth century *Llanelli Ware* faded away. The potters, unable to face the competition from the now highly-mechanised industry in Stoke-on-Trent, simply went out of business. *Llanelli Ware* thus became sought after by collectors including Susan, whose own collection was used as the inspiration for reviving this fine tradition. *Welsh Dresser* is not a slavish imitation of old pieces but a continuation of the popular folk art. In 1992, Angharad Menna created fresh versions in rich colours from the traditional motifs which were then reproduced as transfers for the final designs. With regular introductions of new shapes and colours on tableware, giftware, vases, plant pots, cookware and accessories, Discontinued in 2000, *Welsh Dresser* was one of Portmeirion's most diverse designs, proving popular with customers in the United States, United Kingdom and particularly in Wales. The introduction of a design with a handpainted appearance heralded the introduction of true handpainted designs in 1993.

Queen's Award for Export

In 1990 Portmeirion Pottery (Holdings) plc, was awarded the Silver Jubilee Queen's Award for Export. The award was presented by the Lord Lieutenant of Staffordshire, Sir Arthur Bryan, in a ceremony at the firm's London Road headquarters. Most of the 540 employees joined the special guests in a warehouse at the factory to see Euan Cooper-Willis receive the award and certificate on behalf of the company.

Portmeirion were selling to 34 countries, including America, Italy, Spain, Australia and Canada – Japan, however, was proving a difficult market due to the Japanese preference for fine china. During the ceremony Sir Arthur praised Susan and Euan for their efforts in creating such a successful company. The Queen's Award came during a busy year for Portmeirion Pottery; in January, it acquired the Naugatuck Triangle Corporation, previously an equal partner in Portmeirion U.S.A. This was followed by the purchase of the Sylvac factory to meet the demand for increased production capacity. Following a period of recession in the Potteries, Portmeirion was performing far better than many of their rivals with a turnover increasing by 60% on the previous year. Despite these successes, Portmeirion's management decided that the key to success was in developing their export markets as increasing home sales were proving difficult. These fears proved well founded when a strong pound resulted in falling exports in the mid- to late-nineties.

Handpainting at Portmeirion Pottery

Margaret Brian, one of Portmeirion's lithographers, recognised the potential of the undecorated wares in the Sylvac factory. She had been a hand-paintress for Wedgwood prior to joining Portmeirion and suggested to Works Director, Kami Farhadi, that she try some of her own handpainted designs on the Sylvac pieces. Kami agreed and Margaret was given space in the Longton Factory to set up Portmeirion's handpainting department. For six months, she painted a series of trial mug designs, working alone apart from the occasional assistance of Kami's wife Shahrzad Forouzan, until a range of designs were ready to be unveiled to the public.

Handpainting **Magnolia,** *designed by Angharad Menna, 1996.*

Lane Delph

At the 1992 Harrogate Trade Fair the first examples of *Lane Delph* were shown to prospective buyers. It had been agreed that the new handpainted line would not be sold under the Portmeirion name and that no existing Portmeirion shapes were to be used. Thus only a new nine-ounce 'BF' mug and various existing vase, bowl and pomander shapes were decorated with Margaret's designs of flowers, and a range of brightly-coloured chickens. The official launch under the brand *Lane Delph* was scheduled for August 1992. The following month orders for the new line were flooding in and Margaret was able to take on another skilled paintress, Debbie Wood. Over the next six years, Debbie was the first recruit to what was to become a team of skilled handpaintresses known affectionately as the 'Longton Ladies' and including: Margaret Brian, Debbie Wood, Helen Cash, Zoe Wilson, Helen Cooper, Janet Clee, Lucy Tiler, Amanda Bowles, Dawn Porter, Sue Carter, Naomi Wilson, Julie Edwards. Each paintress had their own individual mark.

Portmeirion Handpainted

Although Margaret did not use Portmeirion shapes for the *Lane Delph* range she did ask Kami for some plates to decorate for her own use, as she had just bought a new kitchen and wanted to paint a dinner service to match her colour scheme. Kami sent over a number of biscuitware Drum-shaped plates which Margaret painted with a simple mandarin orange and leaf design. She sent the plates back to Stoke to be fired but they were never returned. She heard nothing further until an order arrived from John Lewis. Their central china buyer, Mrs Elizabeth Mahon, had seen Margaret's plates in Portmeirion's Stoke showroom during a visit in June 1993 and had fallen in love with them. Thus the first official Portmeirion handpainted design *Mandarin* was launched as a John Lewis exclusive in January 1994. As with many of Portmeirion's designs, events snowballed. A buyer from Harrods saw *Mandarin* and wanted something 'similar but different' so Margaret produced *Lemon Grove*, (still being manufactured in 1999 long after the official withdrawal of handpainted items in 1997). By the end of 1994 Margaret had also designed *Orchard Fruits* for Lawleys and *Peach Tree* for Associated Independent Stores.

Botanic Handpainted

In November 1993, the Portmeirion Collectors Club offered its members a handpainted version of the *Botanic Garden Christmas Rose* motif on a ten-inch plate in a presentation box. Described as a completely new design-approach by Portmeirion and developed exclusively for their Club, handpainted versions did not prove popular next to the familiar print versions of the *Botanic* design. Therefore, plans for further handpainted plates the following year in both *Botanic Garden* and *Pomona* were shelved.

Pugh Brothers

Mandarin was not stocked by John Lewis until January 1994, so the honour of retailing the first Portmeirion handpainted design went to a family firm in South Wales. In 1993 furnishers, Pugh Brothers of Llanelli, commissioned Portmeirion Pottery to revive one of the classic designs of the world-famous Llanelli Pottery to mark their 100th year in the town. The distinctive cockerel motif was the best-known of the many designs to emerge from the local kilns during its heyday (1840-1922). This followed the design painted in the early 1900s by 'Auntie Sal', Sarah Roberts, the only decorator believed to have painted these cockerels. The original birds faced to the left, with a distinctive blue-sponged border. The new design was copied from an original piece in the Parc Howard Museum, Llanelli. The *Celiog Llanelly* (*Lanelli Cockerel*) plate was the brainchild of John Pugh (the director of Pugh Brothers), a grandson of the original brothers who founded the business in 1893. He originally commissioned 750 plates, but these had been sold within four weeks of their appearance so an even larger order was placed to cope with the Christmas rush. The range was soon expanded from just plates and mugs to jugs, teapots, store jars, planters and fruit bowls.

The design was initially produced in two versions *Brown* and *Blue Cockerel* but the blue version proved far more popular so the brown was discontinued. Production problems were also found with the sponged border. Sponging cobalt blue onto the biscuit ware resulted in drips and finger marks which only became apparent when the pieces were fired. This technique was dropped in favour of a far more efficient floral border. A second *Llanelli Ware* design *Rhosyn Glâs* (*Blue Rose*) had been introduced by November 1993, and resembled a monochrome version of Angharad Menna's *Welsh Dresser* pattern introduced the previous year. Both handpainted designs were continually supplied to Pugh Brothers until the handpainting department was closed. With the success of the new designs under the Portmeirion name it was decided to discontinue production of handpainted items under the *Lane Delph* name and to concentrate on developing a new range, *Portmeirion Studio,* which could be sold through existing Portmeirion outlets.

Portmeirion Studio

Two designs were developed by Margaret Brian for release in 1994, *Sweet Pea* by Angharad Menna, and *Summer Fruits*. The latter mirrored the designs that had been so successful as department store exclusives, but the totally new *Sweet Pea* motif was not so successful and was discontinued in 1996 when a floral dinnerware design *Magnolia* by Angharad Menna, and a kitchen range *Kitchen Garden* by Debbie Wood, were introduced. *Magnolia* was marked as being designed exclusively for the Royal Botanical Gardens in Kew but was also available through Portmeirion's other stockists. *Kitchen Garden* was a very striking, naive design of vegetables on a white ground. Peppers, onions and carrots appeared on a variety of store jars and serving bowls. Debbie Wood's skill as a designer is better seen in her exclusive design *Barn Yard* which she produced for the Midlands-based china chain, James The Second. *Barn Yard* is a colourful collection of farm animals showing a real sense of fun, a duck, sheep, pig, cat, cow and chicken, are worked on a range of simple cups and bowls. Debbie's sense of humour is also seen in her *Dolphin* design which was used on a range of bathroom accessories. Trials were also produced by other members of the Portmeirion design team: *Aztec* a multicoloured cross-hatch pattern by Julian Teed, and a variety of patterns by Angharad Menna including a collection of the statues in Portmeirion village executed in a combination of sponge prints with handpainted detail, an idea that was later transferred to a fabric design for the village.

By 1997 Margaret Brian was convinced that the quality of the work being produced by her department was superior to anything available in the United Kingdom. However, following two years of falling sales across the ranges (part of a general recession in the Staffordshire Industry), Portmeirion's Chief Executive, Mary-Lorraine Hughes, announced the closure of the hand-painting department in the spring of 1997 as part of a major re-structuring of the company, though Portmeirion continued to supply orders from Harrods for *Lemon Grove*.

Angharad Menna, Susan and Euan's daughter, is a consultant designer for Portmeirion Pottery.

Cardew Teapots

In 1993 Portmeirion joined in partnership with Devon-based collectable teapot manufacturers, Cardew Design, investing in 15% of the newly-formed company. Cardew's co-founder and chief designer, Paul Cardew, has won many awards for his unique ceramic sculptures.

Cardew teapots are purely decorative – the first was the *Portmeirion China Stall* introduced to members of the Collectors Club in November 1993, retailing at £79.95. Incorporated into the pot were miniature Portmeirion shapes decorated with tiny versions of *Botanic Garden* transfers, each teapot reported to take over seven days to make. In March 1994, three more teapots were added: L/S (large size) *Washstand* and *Victorian Tea Table* and its diminutive namesake, the first of the S/S (small size), *Victorian Tea Table* which retailed at £21.95. *Kitchen Sink,* and the most expensive *Dresser* teapot retailing at £99.95, were added for 1994 as well as more S/S versions, so that all the large pots had a smaller sibling.

A pair of novelty brooches was also made by Cardew in 1994 in the shape of tiny *Botanic Garden* tea and coffee pots at £6.95 each including a simple but effective decorated 'pillbox'-shaped presentation box. Two teapots were introduced exclusively for America in 1996 using decorated lids on a traditional Green Betty base. Two lids were available with *Botanic Garden* miniatures, *Picnic* featuring a thermos flask and hamper, and *Gardening* with trowel and plant pots. Large and small celebration pots were also introduced to the main range along with the option of *Pomona* as well as *Botanic* motifs and by 1997 twenty-four teapots were available to United Kingdom collectors with prices ranging from £25.50 to £110. A miniature, green, wooden display dresser was also available but was too small to hold the entire range. From 1997, Cardew continued and extended the range of Portmeirion *Botanic Garden* collectable teapots under licence to Portmeirion Pottery, distributed with a Cardew backstamp.

Portmeirion China

Portmeirion China was launched in February 1994 at the International Spring Fair held at Birmingham's National Exhibition Centre. This was the result of a lengthy research programme by Portmeirion's Technical Director Philip White to develop a material with the aesthetic appeal of bone china and the strength and characteristics of porcelain. The result, *Portmeirion China,* was a revolutionary rethink of the traditional recipe for English bone china. It contained no animal bone (unlike true bone china which could contain as much as 50%), and yet had the major advantages of bone china and porcelain, being very white and translucent, of oven-to-table quality and highly resistant to chipping. To complement the exceptional qualities of 'Portmeirion China' Susan Williams-Ellis designed a simple but classically elegant shape which she named Moonstone. Portmeirion's designers initially developed five new designs for the shape: *Ladies Flower Garden* (1994-2000), *Summer Garland* (1994-99), *Ancestral Jewels* (1994-99), *Welsh Wild Flowers* (1994-2000), and *Moonstone Gold* (1994-95).

In the autumn of 1995 a range of decorative giftware, including a Vienna clock and an eleven-inch ginger jar, was added to existing Portmeirion China tableware. These shapes were used in 1998 as the basis of the *Botanic Garden China Giftware Collection* which used the larger *Botanic* motifs to great effect. Other china exclusives were also produced for various department stores, and as collectors' items. Private commissions were undertaken for The National Trust and The Royal Botanic Gardens, Kew, for whom Portmeirion produced a magnificent boxed teacup and saucer set with a special floral transfer and gilding to commemorate the opening of The Japanese Landscape Garden in 1996.

Midsummer Night

Predating all other Portmeirion China designs but still on Susan's Moonstone body, *Midsummer Night* a trial motif by Julian Teed, the Product Development Director, was developed in 1992 for the export market. A striking effect is achieved by mounting an array of common English garden flowers on a jet black background.

Ladies Flower Garden

Derived from a book of the same name by Mrs Loudon, c1842, a total of eighteen bouquets of flowers was carefully chosen for this 1994 design, and arranged by Susan and her daughter Anwyl. The beautiful, hand-coloured original illustrations were meticulously reproduced in twenty-one colours. The pattern is completed by a border of twisted ribbon.

Summer Garland

A collection of some of the favourite flower motifs from Portmeirion's well-known *Botanic Garden* pattern are woven into a luxuriant wreath. Originally an accessory design to complement *Botanic Garden.*

Welsh Wild Flowers

The very detailed, botanically accurate watercolours of Welsh hillside flowers by Angharad Menna, are carefully arranged on the china. The effect is fresh and contemporary.

Ancestral Jewels

Designed by Anwyl Cooper-Willis and inspired by ancient Celtic jewellery, this 1994 pattern has a richness which contrasts with the floral designs. Bands of historic jewellery border the ware and gold highlights the richness of the design.

Moonstone Gold

Hand finishing with a simple band of 22 carat gold, was used with great effect to show the beauty of the Moonstone shape. However, the high production cost

Julian Teed, Product Development Director, Portmeirion Pottery.

Anwyl Cooper-Willis, Susan and Euan's daughter, Design Director at Portmeirion Pottery.

could not be justified and within twelve months the design had been withdrawn.

Portmeirion Marble

Portmeirion Marble by Susan Williams-Ellis is a simple but expensive-looking border pattern intended for the Italian market. Stone textures are presented in a mix and match contemporary colourways in this exclusively dinnerware range. Each item was available in yellow, dark blue, light blue, maroon, sea green or pink.

Fine Fruits

The Fine Fruits Collection was launched as a Debenhams exclusive just in time for the 1998 Christmas season. Using smaller versions of the *Pomona* motifs, each item in this range of tableware was complemented by a border of fine, green banding. The design was discontinued by Debenhams in the spring of 1999 but Portmeirion continued to market the design under the name *Pomona China.*

The Portmeirion Collectors Club

In July 1993, the first issue of Portmeirion Collectors Club News was sent out to the fledgling membership formed from Portmeirion's customers who had either been sent, or found one of the Pottery's Collectors Club fliers available free from Portmeirion retailers. This included the following message from the Pottery's founders:

> Dear Collector,
>
> Since I formed Portmeirion Potteries with my husband, Euan Cooper-Willis, thirty or so years ago, we have seen the company develop into an internationally renowned business. The company was initially formed to produce pottery for our gift shop in the village of Portmeirion which my father, Sir Clough Williams-Ellis, created in 1926. Now a place of historic and architectural importance, the village is a major tourist attraction. During these years we have witnessed the development of a loyal group of collectors world wide, who have shown a tremendous interest in the company and its products. As acknowledgement of this loyalty and to encourage new collectors, we have launched the 'Portmeirion Collectors Club'. The club will provide members with more information regarding the company's history, designs and products, some of which will be exclusively available to Club members. The Club's first exclusive item will be a Botanic Garden Small Mantle Clock, including a Collectors' Club backstamp. Only a limited number will be produced so order now to avoid disappointment. The first year's subscription will be £15.00 in return for which you will receive your own membership pack along with entitlement to Club benefits.
>
> MEMBERSHIP BENEFITS: Complimentary Gifts, Portmeirion Book of Entertainment, Cake Set and Membership Card to signify that you are an official Club Member. Newsletter Information regarding the company and exclusive offers available to members will be sent at regular intervals. We look-forward to welcoming you as an official member of the Portmeirion Collectors' Club.
>
> Yours sincerely, Susan Williams-Ellis

Once word was spread by retailers, membership of the Portmeirion Collectors Club grew to today's figure of around 10,000. Although the main function of the Club is as a marketing aid for Portmeirion to keep their loyal customers informed about new products, the benefits of joining are always worth the subscription fee. The Club Secretaries, Lisa Champ (1993-96) and Dawn Shufflebotham (1996 to present), have both been available to answer queries about Portmeirion and offer a high-quality customer service. A wide variety of exclusive items have been offered to members throughout the years of the club's existence and have included unique items such as the handpainted *Botanic Garden* 10-inch plate (1993).

A charming miniature china box in the shape of an egg was commissioned exclusively for the Club in 1994. In 1995 to celebrate the 35th anniversary of the founding of Portmeirion Pottery, a specially commissioned *Coral Jug* was produced. A standard version was made for general sales and another with a special inscription exclusively for collectors. Other items have also been offered to collectors including the discontinued *Punch* and *Jewel* British Heritage jugs and the *Enchanted Garden* range. Examples of the truly exclusive Collectors Club items rarely come up for sale and are avidly sort after by those who missed the original offers. Collectors Club events, held in department stores throughout the United Kingdom, provide a friendly environment where collectors can meet and learn more about Portmeirion from the staff themselves.

Christmas Ornaments

To coincide with the creation of the Portmeirion Collectors Club and Portmeirion China, in 1992 the factory produced the first of its dated *Christmas Ornaments*, better known as the *Christmas Bells*, miniature china bells threaded with a green ribbon ideal for hanging from Christmas trees. Combining *Botanic Garden* with traditional holly motifs, the first holiday souvenir was joined in 1993 by the first of an equally successful series of *Christmas Plates*. Plates and bells are supplied in their own green, satin-lined presentation boxes making an ideal gift item. The launch of a new bell and plate has now become an annual event amongst collectors who look forward to the announcement of the year's featured flowers. The success of the *Christmas Bell* as a tree decoration obviously inspired Portmeirion to produce other miniature *Christmas Ornaments* including various undated china bells, miniature tureens, tea and coffee pots all with green ribbons. The success of these may also have helped in Portmeirion's decision to introduce their 1995 range of dinnerware devoted to the holiday season, *The Holly and The Ivy*.

Botanic Garden Christmas Plates

1993 Christmas Rose	1994 Shrubby Peony
1995 Chrysanthemum	1996 Virgin's Bower
1997 Passion Flower	1998 Honeysuckle
1999 Lily Flowered Azalea	

Botanic Garden Xmas Ornaments (Bells)

1992 Rhododendron	1993 Cyclamen
1994 Daisy	1995 Heartsease
1996 Trailing Bindweed	1997 Pimpernel
1998 Snow-Drop & Crocus	1999 Speedwell

Portmeirion USA

The mid-1980s saw an improvement in Portmeirion's fortunes following a recession a decade earlier. In 1984 the company's turnover increased from two to four million. Annual growth continued at 60% for the following four years, thanks in part to the launch of Portmeirion U.S.A. which was founded in 1996 as a joint venture between Naugatuck Triangle Corporation and Portmeirion Potteries. Naugatuck was the parent company of S. P. Skinner Company Inc. and the Pintail Corporation, distributors of fine home decorative accessories and gifts. Portmeirion shared a showroom on Fifth Avenue, New York, with Skinner and Pintail, their merchandise was stored and shipped from Skinner's warehouse in Naugatuck, Connecticut. Portmeirion chose the American company as a proven track record in servicing the American Market was needed to meet their objectives of expanding their distribution to cover the United States more evenly and to serve their customers more efficiently. Portmeirion Pottery Ltd., was profitable but, again, they found that they did not have the capital to invest in the new equipment and staff required to meet the demands of an ever-increasing order book. To remedy this, in 1988 Portmeirion went public. With a turnover of £20 million, the shares were issued at £1.80 and soon reached £2.10. Combined with a second issue, this generated enough capital to finance a major expansion. In 1990, the newly-named, Portmeirion Pottery Holdings plc, bought Sylvac's factory, the Sylvian Works at Longton, Stoke-on-Trent. Although the old factory and a newly-built extension were intended for the production of cast hollow ware pottery the building was still filled with Sylvac's equipment and wares in various stages of production. Amongst the treasure trove were Sylvac's archive of block moulds dating back many years. Susan went through these master-copies of the shapes, prior to their storage to see if any were of use to Portmeirion. Amongst the many animal figures and novelty containers she found only one classic shape, a Neptune vase design, which was ideal for the British Heritage Collection.

Portmeirion Publications

With so many family and professional links to the industry it was not surprising that Portmeirion should eventually become publishers. The *Portmeirion Book of Country Cooking* in 1988, combined recipes from the world famous Portmeirion Hotel with lavish photographs of the dishes on Portmeirion pottery. This format was continued in 1990 with the *Portmeirion Book of Entertaining* and in 1995 with the *Portmeirion Book of Feasts and Festivals* which also

Susan at work on a new shape, 1999.

Kami Farhardi is the Chief Executive of Portmeirion Potteries.

includes attractive line drawings by Susan Williams-Ellis of her favourite *Botanic* and *Pomona* motifs. Two handy little editions were issued in 1992, the *Portmeirion Recipe Notebook* and the *Portmeirion Address Book*. In 1995 to coincide with the 35th Anniversary of the factory *The Story of Portmeirion Potteries 1960 - 1995 (A Collectors Guide 1995)*, was compiled by Victoria Stanton with Euan Cooper-Willis. This book introduced collectors to many long-forgotten designs. Following the success of this pocket book, the 25th anniversary of *Botanic Garden* was also marked with a commemorative guide and in 1997 *The World of Botanic Garden* was sent out to Collectors Club members and included in boxed sets of commemorative china. This tiny volume proved an invaluable guide to discontinued designs and uncovered a forgotten history, and copies are available from Portmeirion distributors.

Publications

Portmeirion Book of Country Cooking 1988
Portmeirion Book of Entertaining 1990
Portmeirion Address Book 1992
Portmeirion Recipe Notebook 1992
Portmeirion Book of Feasts & Festivals 1995
The Story of Portmeirion Potteries 1960 - 1995
A Collectors Guide 1995
The World of Botanic Garden 1997

Harvest Blue

Blue and white pottery such as the long-established *Blue Holland* has always been popular so Portmeirion launched their own twist on a traditional delph-like motif on a range of dinnerware in February 1995. *Harvest Blue* was designed by Susan's daughter Angharad Menna, and based on the traditions of eighteenth-century Dutch still life painting. The *Harvest Blue* motif was described as, 'giving the feel of an old established orchard where flowers are planted among the fruit trees and roses tangle with the vines'. The combination of the traditional monochrome motif and the Romantic shape produced a range of wares that made a refreshing change from the colourful fruits and flowers then associated with Portmeirion. The number of items available in *Harvest Blue* grew steadily over the next few years, incorporating chopping boards, fabrics and bathroom sets. In July 1996, plain-centred plates were introduced in response to Italian demands for a more subtle use of the motif. Despite the popularity amongst its band of loyal collectors, sales were disappointing and in February 1999, *Harvest Blue* was withdrawn from Portmeirion's price list, transfer stocks to be held for matching until February 2004.

The Victorian Cook's Collection

This decorative kitchenware was described in promotional material as 'a light hearted design for serious cooks', *The Victorian Cook's Collection* by Anwyl Cooper-Willis was launched at the Harrogate Gift Show in July 1996. The *Cook's* motifs were inspired by a Victorian cook's scrap book – including nifty gadgets, useful thoughts and novel dishes for elaborate dinner parties, and to create an atmosphere of creativity in the kitchen. Mrs Beeton's *Book of Home Management* was one obvious source of inspiration – typical Victorian book illustrations and descriptions in a fine copper-plate hand were faithfully reproduced in a dark green, with a fashionable sea-green tone to lift the images and add a little colour to the pattern. There was only a limited number of items in the range but there was a collection of accessories, oven gloves etc. with matching images and a green trim. The Staffordshire jugs are attractive items from the set. Unfortunately, only a year earlier, Portmeirion had discontinued its long running rolling pins and sugar shakers, two items which may have added to what was a very limited range: a 9-inch mixing bowl, store jars, Staffordshire jugs and large serving pieces, with plates also introduced after the launch. During this period, Angharad Menna had introduced a similar design of randomly scattered images of Portmeirion village's architectural features in a similar colour range as a fabric motif. A year later Susan introduced her version of the *Botanic Garden* fabric, using images from the design and called the *Indoor Garden Collection*.

The Holly and the Ivy

Named after and featuring the lyrics of the popular English carol of the 1600s, Anwyl Cooper-Willis' 1996 design is a contemporary arrangement of antique illustrations surrounded by a flowing script. Originally launched as an 'American Holiday' exclusive it also proved popular in the United Kingdom when it was released for general sale in 1997. Again on the Drum shape, *The Holly and the Ivy* has a sophisticated and original design which, although intended to stand alone, may also be used to add a seasonal touch when mixed and matched with *Botanic Garden*. As well as dinnerware, *The Holly and the Ivy* has also been used on accessories as the only coloured motif on United Kingdom Portmeirion glass and on one of the last of Portmeirion's miniature collectors' teapots.

China Miniature Hinged Boxes

These miniatures follow the tradition of European porcelain boxes and those made by Chelsea in the mid eighteenth century. Portmeirion's characteristic shapes, so readily recognisable, were ideal for adapting to this format. Made out of white, translucent Portmeirion China mounted with gilded hinges and decorated with minutely detailed prints, these boxes, introduced in May 1996, were an attractive gift item. A lovely revival of an eighteenth-century idea, the china box range, comprised six of Portmeirion's most famous shapes and were decorated exactly like their full-size counterparts in the two best-loved patterns, *Botanic Garden* and *Pomona*.

Enamelled Box Range

The art of enamelling was known in the classical Greek and Etruscan world, and has been used to decorate precious objects ever since. The technique of painting enamels was introduced to Britain by French craftsmen in the fifteenth century but copper-enamelled trinkets or toys did not become popular until about 1740. Portmeirion's enamels introduced in 1996, were made in much the same way as those of the eighteenth century. The box was shaped from copper, then three individual layers of enamel were fired on. Once the enamel base was prepared the decoration was applied in the form of a transfer and the whole thing was fired once more. The enamel box components were then hand-mounted onto a gilded hinge and the piece was complete. These boxes were available in the six *Pomona* fruits (apple, pear, plum, cherry, peach and red currant). In *Botanic Garden* the decorations had been arranged to follow the eighteen plates in the *Botanic Garden* range; the two large sizes came with the 6 ten-inch plate motifs, the medium with 6 eight-inch plate motifs and the small with 6 six-inch plate motifs. Both ranges were discontinued in 1999.

The Enchanted Garden

Susan had long wanted to share her favourite childhood pictures with today's children, and so produced this special nursery set in 1997, decorated with scenes from *In Fairyland* illustrated by Richard Doyle (a nephew of Sir Arthur Conan Doyle, creator of Sherlock Holmes, whose original illustrations were first published in the mid-nineteenth century.) Some of the illustrations had been engraved for use on nursery ware in the early sixties, black prints with hand colouring and banded details in pink, blue and gold. These were produced on some of Susan's early shapes and were made until 1963/4. Susan's grandmother had a copy of this book and the two would often look at it together, discussing events in the fairy world and finding some new tiny detail at which to marvel. When Susan became an artist, her grandmother gave her the book and it became one of her most treasured possessions, bringing back memories of happy times. The book disappeared from the factory in the sixties and the same copy was later found again by Susan in an antiquarian book shop in Stoke! Boxed sets were advertised as an inexpensive gift item in 1961, a relief plate with an alphabet border being the central piece. These sets were exhibited at the same time as *Dolphin* and *Malachite*. This recent treatment of Richard Doyle's designs, called *The Enchanted Garden,* reproduces in sensitive colours the great snail race, elves and owls' games, butterflies and fairy princesses and, according to promotional literature:

> The collection provides ideal presents for new additions to the family and for good children at Christmas time and birthdays .

A promotional video was also produced for the American market with Susan reading the stories to her great grandchildren. The design was withdrawn in 1999.

Swinging Ceramics

As a tribute to Susan Williams-Ellis who celebrated her eightieth birthday on the 6th of June 1998, The Potteries Museum and Art Gallery in association with Portmeirion Pottery, created a display entitled 'Swinging Ceramics - Susan Williams-Ellis and Portmeirion Pottery 1960-82. From May 29th to September 27th 1998, a collection of over sixty items, housed in two display cases, could be seen in the foyer of The Potteries Museum and Art Gallery, Bethesda Street, Hanley, Stoke-on-Trent. The display was prepared by Kathy Niblett who in 1982, with her husband Paul, had written the book *Hand-Painted Gray's Pottery*. The items displayed included a number of trial items borrowed from Portmeirion's archive, designs from the mid 1960s, and followed the development of Portmeirion Pottery up to *Botanic Garden* and the introduction of the Romantic shape in the early 1980s. A colourful guide and poster were designed for the exhibition featuring a variety of the factory's output.

Options

At February's International Spring Fair in Birmingham 1998, a new addition to the *Botanic Garden* range called *Options* was launched to enthusiastic reviews. This was a range of complementary pieces that could be mixed and matched with existing *Botanic Garden* items, enabling a change of style in table setting to suit the mood or occasion required. The concept was to add a little late twentieth-century minimalism to the *Botanic Garden* range with pared down, non-floral designs. The pieces that comprise the range are: a 13-inch Italian green glass charger plate deeply engraved with the distinctive leaf border, intended to retail at £14.50, and two undecorated

Susan with Jools Holland opening the Portmeirion garden at Chelsea Flower Show, 1999.

Grazyna Whittle is a freelance designer who produced illustrations for the **Seasons** *Collection.*

white plates with an embossed leaf border, (the ten-inch at £7.50 and the eight-inch at £5.95). To add to the tableware two deep-cut crystal glasses and three frosted glass beakers (or vases) complemented the place settings, which also featured the engraved leaf border. *Options* also included green or white napkins and tablecloths with a textured lattice pattern and sparing use of butterflies and flowers. The same design was used on the *Botanic Garden* wallpaper used in Portmeirion village. The most unusual addition to this minimalist range is a green glass napkin ring in the shape of a flower - a number of these Italian glass flowers were also produced with long stems purely for decorative use on retailers displays. Saatchi's press advertisements for *Options* with the caption 'Portmeirion - A Plate With A Flower On It' won much critical acclaim and was nominated for a number of advertising awards. *Options* was carried in the United Kingdom by Debenhams stores who also had promotional eight-inch plates made as an alternative to the usual in-store point of sale plaques.

Millennium Rose

For many years Susan Williams-Ellis' friend, rosarian David Austin, had repeatedly offered to have a rose named after Portmeirion. Susan had declined the offer but in 1999 she considered the time for the rose had arrived. For the 1999 Chelsea Flower Show, Portmeirion, in association with Wyevale Garden Centres, was planning a garden which took its styling cues from Portmeirion village and for which David Austin was approached to produce a 'Portmeirion Rose'. Susan who had already been working on a variety of rose designs planned to create a motif based on the rose for a series of limited edition millennium collectors' items – all the projects were to be ready for the opening of the four-day flower show on the 18th of May 1999. For a few short days in May, a dramatic 40-foot tower dominated the skyline on the banks of the Thames by the Battersea Bridge in London. The tower was a copy of the Camera Obscura which overlooks the harbour of Portmeirion village in North Wales. It formed the centrepiece of the award-winning Wyevale/Portmeirion Garden designed by Chelsea Flower Show veterans Bunny Guinness and Peter Eustance. The Portmeirion garden was officially opened by pianist and Portmeirion aficionado Jools Holland holding a giant pair of scissors with a keyboard motif on the blades, assisted by Susan Williams-Ellis. Immediately after the opening Susan presented Jools with the very limited edition '1 of 1' Portmeirion *Millennium Rose* china salad bowl thus marking the launch of Portmeirion's *Millennium Collection*. Selected items of the *Portmeirion Rose Collection* were available from Wyevale Garden Centres, Debenhams and selected Portmeirion stockists. Debenhams stores boasted three exclusive items; a limited edition nine-inch luncheon plate, an unlimited edition china bell, and a large candle with rose petals embedded in the wax. Although many branches of Debenhams did not stock the Millennium items, those that did soon found the limited edition items selling fast and stocks running low by September. To fill the gaps on Debenhams shelves, Portmeirion released a series of three, inexpensive, twelve-inch, ten-inch and eight-inch, *Botanic Garden* Millennium plates featuring the three new *Botanic Garden* plate motifs and the phrase 'A New Millennium - The Year 2000'. Some Debenhams stores also received non-limited edition plates featuring the smallest *Millennium Rose* roundel surrounded by four rose buds instead of the single large roundel seen on the limited

Jo Gorman is a staff designer at Portmeirion Potteries and is responsible for the new **Dusk** *design.*

Julie Ingham is a freelance designer who produced **Dawn** *for Portmeirion Potteries.*

edition plates. This and other *Millennium Rose* trial items appeared in Portmeirion's Second Shops during the Winter of 1999/2000 extending the *Millennium Collection* to over thirty items.

Seasons Collection

With some of Portmeirion's competitors going out of business, in the late 1990s, hard decisions had to be made to ensure the future of the company. Having accepted that variations on *Botanic Garden* and *Pomona* could not sustain the Pottery indefinitely, and given the comparative commercial failures of other designs introduced after 1972, Portmeirion took outside advice to find a new product to carry them forward. Towards the end of 1997, design partnership Queensberry Hunt Levien was contracted for a nine-month period. Recognising that it is always difficult to follow a success, they encouraged Portmeirion to change direction from the archival design of *Botanic Garden* and to think in a more creative way. Queensberry Hunt Levien used their experience to advise on future trends in the ceramics market, helped to find designers, explain what colours should be used and point the way for Portmeirion to launch a new range. In June 1998, halfway through Queensberry Hunt Levien's period at Portmeirion, Dr. Mary Lorraine Hughes resigned. Kami Farhadi took over as Group Chief Executive and one month later replaced the head of Portmeirion U.S.A. In February 1999, the result of Portmeirion's work with Queensberry Hunt Levien was unveiled with a completely new range of tableware and accessories called the *Seasons Collection*. This was inspired by natural forms 'the moods of nature' with a soft feel and pastel colour palette. Research had shown the need for informal dinnerware to cater for a new lifestyle suitable for today's relaxed entertaining. The range is therefore compact but complemented by accessories in slate, concrete and aluminium with the leaf motif carried through on many of the pieces. An eclectic array of glassware, candles, tablecloths, napkins and runners in cotton organdie or a heavier damask complete the range. Mugs, tiny butter pats, casserole dishes and a large selection of bowls add to the traditional teaware items to form the largest collection the factory has produced in fifteen years. Two styles were launched, *Seasons' Leaves* and *Seasons' Flowers,* both designed to have a calm and peaceful look on the five pastel background colours (blue, beige, green, cream and lilac). However, by the end of 1999 it was clear that outlets were stocking the *Leaves* rather than the more figurative and traditional *Flowers. The Seasons Collection* was very much a team effort - the Mandarin shape was modelled by Susan Williams-Ellis with geometric lines and curves harking back to her work of the mid-1960s. Susan's daughters, Angharad Menna and Anwyl Cooper-Willis, contributed designs and with Julian Teed coordinated the whole collection.

Dawn and Dusk

Two new designs on the Mandarin shape followed the *Seasons Collection* and were launched at Birmingham in Spring 2000. *Dawn* is a soft-toned pattern by textile designer Julie Ingham. The design consists of bands of different patterns each with a different feel, that work together to form a contemporary colour scheme on the modern-shaped ware. Additional interest is created during the printing process where subtle texture is created in the shape of seeds or tiny flower heads while other seed heads are finely drawn on another section of the design. Coordinating items once again broaden the appeal of this design. *Dusk* continues the bold motifs of the *Seasons Collection* and utilises deep, rich colours in contrast to its partner pattern. 'Midnight' and 'aubergine' glazes are used on lids and the outside of bowls, and are carried through to coordinating pearlised glassware. Jo Gorman, Portmeirion's in-house designer, has used tinted skeletal leaf forms, singly or grouped, in a darker palette than *Seasons* to pattern the ware, inspired by 'the colours of nature at dusk'. Soft watercolour backgrounds add contemporary 'interior designer' colour to the design. The glaze colours were softened to fit American market trends.

At the Birmingham Trade Fair in 1999 the *Seasons* collection displayed on the stunning Portmeirion stand took one's breath away – a double take – but it's Portmeirion! Already there are copyists.

This new design direction has been revolutionary, but *Botanic Garden* is part of our culture and will be with us for a long time.

Pattern Listings

Gray's Pottery

Patterns Susan designed or continued producing after the takeover in 1960.

Welsh Scenes
Shells
Sailing Ships
Masonic
Dolphin
Riverboats
London Prints

Kirkham's Pottery

To the end of 1961, also marked 'Old Staffordshire'. (Unmarked Portmeirion items may be Kirkham pieces.)

Historic medical and scientific equipment
Staffordshire Dogs, Hens and Jugs
Mortars and Pestles
Hospital chamber pots, inhalers etc.
Apothecary jars with sprigs and flowers or full-colour Pratt Prints
Safari – black and white chefs with yellow and red enamel detail
Red banded kitchenware with white polka dots
Acid dishes
Thomas Bewick illustrations
White Horse Whisky jug and ashtray

Portmeirion Ware (Gray's Pottery 1960-62)

Dolphin continued from Gray's in lustre or coloured grounds
Knights – on ground layed orange, taupe, or black on white
Malachite 1960
Moss Agate 1961
Gold Diamond 1961
Black Diamond 1961
Gold Sun 1961
Cornucopia 1962
Talisman 1962
Tiger Lily 1962
Portmeirion Rose and other assorted florals with or without coloured banding

Portmeirion Pottery 1962+

Medicine Prints 1962 renamed *Chemist Prints* in 1965
Potted Game
Allan Line
Volunteers
Circassian Beauties
Pantomime Characters 1966
Favorite Horseman 1966
British Herald 1966
Mississippi Riverboats 1962+
Bewick – *Country Life/Sporting Scenes*
Blue Holland (open-stock transfer)
Black Key/Greek Key 1963
Gold Lion 1963
Totem 1963
Jupiter 1964
Samarkand 1964
Shakespeare 1964
Cypher 1964
Variations 1964
Tivoli 1964
Shells colour screen print 1965
Jewel 1965
Fortuna 1965
Corsets 1965
Monte Sol 1965
Gold Six 1965
Chemist Prints 1965 (colour version of black and white prints)
Magic City 1966
Reddington's New Foot Soldiers 1967
Lapidaire Alphabet 1968
Gold Brocades 1968
Lovely Ladies 1968
Zodiac 1968
Phoenix 1968
What Shall I Drink? 1969
Suitable Sentiments 1968
Great Occasions 1972
Love and Friendship 1972
Useful Notices 1968
Moon Landing 1969
A Year to Remember 1969
Magic Garden 1970
Where Did You Get That Hat? 1970
Idols of the Stage 1970
Queen of Carthage 1970
Mayflower Anniversary 1970
HMS Endeavour 1970
Royal Palm 1971
A Year to Remember 1971
Mother's Day 1971-72
Meridian 1971
A Year to Remember 1970
Gold Medallion 1972
Kingdom of the Sea 1972
The Botanic Garden 1972
Blue Garland 1974
Oranges and Lemons 1975
Nursery Balloons 1975 (open-stock)
Birds of Britain 1977
Rose and Passion Flower 1978
Pomona 1980
Summer Strawberries 1980
Variations (Botanic Garden) 1980
Compleat Angler 1981
Romantica 1982
White Almond Blossom (RHS) 1983
Spirit of Christmas 1983
Red Dragon Cookware 1984
Flowers of the Year 1985
The Queen's Hidden Garden 1986
Weeping Hearts 1986
Fluted Whiteware 1987
Welsh Dresser 1992
Novelty Teapots
Holly and Ivy 1995
Harvest Blue 1995
Victorian Cook's Collection 1996
Enchanted Garden 1997
Options 1998
The Seasons Collection 1999
Millennium Rose 1999
Portmeirion Village 75th 2000
Dawn 2000
Dusk 2000
Prisoner mugs 2000

Bathroom Range 1982

Wild Briar
Bridesmaid
Countryside
Fern
Water Lily
Carnation
Poppy
Pansy
Holland

Portmeirion China

Midnight Garden 1992 (trial by Julian Teed)
Moonstone Gold 1994
Ladies Flower Garden 1994
Welsh Wild Flowers 1994
Ancestral Jewel 1994
Summer Garland 1994
Marble 1995
Kew Gardens Japanese Garden 1996
Fine Fruits 1998 (Debenhams)
Botanic Garden China Giftware 1998
Pomona China 1996

British Heritage Collection

Grape 1984
Gothic 1984
Nightingale 1984
Cupid 1985
The Huntsman 1985
The Tournament 1985
George Washington 1986
Hannibal 1986
Cable 1987
Jewel 1987
Mask and Flowers 1987
Pilgrim 1987
Punch and Judy 1987
Arcadia 1988
Water Babies 1998
Hand with Flambeau 1988
Hand with Tulip 1988
Rose Bouquet 1988
Cornucopia 1988
Portland Vase 1989
Pair of Boots 1989
Shepherd 1989
Shepherdess 1989
Swan 1989
Water Carrier, Male 1989
Water Carrier, Female 1989
Babes in the Wood 1990
Grape Harvesters 1990
Neptune Vase 1994
Rose Lamp 1994
Candlesticks 1994

Portmeirion Handpainted

Ceiliog Lannelly (Cockerel) 1993 for Pugh Brothers
Rhosyn Glâs (Blue Rose) 1993 for Pugh Brothers
Lemon Grove 1994 (Harrods)
Peach Tree 1994 (for AIS)
Mandarin 1994 (for John Lewis)
Barn Yard 1996 (for James The Second)
Portmeirion Dolphin 1996
Magnolia 1996 (for Royal Botanic Gardens Kew)
Aztec 1994 (trial)
Tarzan 1994 (trial)

Portmeirion Studio

Sweet Pea 1994
Summer Fruit 1994
Orchard Fruits 1994 (for Lawley's)
Kitchen Garden 1996

Botanic Garden Motifs Guide 1972-1999

During the early 1980s, coinciding with the launch of the *Compleat Angler* a numbering system was introduced to aid the identification of motifs. '*Angler, Birds of Britain* and *Botanic Garden* all had numbers inserted into their transfers. At the same time, the typefaces were changed on the *Botanic* motifs; the Latin names were written in a less formal version of the original classical Roman capitals and the common name was changed from a formal copper-plate to a more readable italic. The number of the design was written in green next to the common or trivial name. With the introduction of more designs, the numbering system for *Botanic Garden* became unmanageable and the numbers were dropped from all new transfers. The original six *Botanic* 'oatmeal motifs' may have been the first motifs to be numbered as an aid to identification in the absence of printed names. The spelling of the Latin names on the list below is taken from the pattern names on the plates.

Key to abbreviated titles of publications:

The Universal Herbal (Botanical, Medical and Agricultural Dictionary), Thomas Green c1824 – Thomas Green c1824
Moral of Flowers by Mrs Hey illustrated by William Clarke, 1835 – William Clarke, 1835
The Botanical Magazine, Vol VI, William Curtis, 1792 – William Curtis, 1792
Medical Botany Vol I, John Stevenson and James Mors Churchill – Stevenson and Churchill
Flora Conspicua (A Selection of the Most Ornamental Flowering, Hardy Exotic Plants for Embellishing Flower Gardens and Pleasure Grounds), Richard Morris. Illustrated by William Clarke, 1830 – William Clarke, 1830
La Flore des Dames, A. Jacquemart, 1840 – A. Jacquemart, 1840

10-inch Dinner Plate Motifs

Dionaea Muscipula – (1) Venus's Fly Trap
Introduced 1973
Replaced by *Clematis Florida* 1995
Original illustration Thomas Green c1824

Amaryllis Reginae – (2) Mexican Lily
Introduced 1973
Replaced by *Flowered Chrysanthemum* 1994
The butterflies were changed 1985 and 1993.
Original illustration Thomas Green c1824

Passiflora Caerulea – (3) Blue Passion Flower
Introduced 1973 –still available
Original illustration William Clarke, 1835

Fritillaria – (4) The Yellow Crown Imperial
Introduced 1973
Replaced by *Christmas Rose* 1984
Original illustration Thomas Green c1824

Hippomane Mancinella – (5) Manchineel Tree
Introduced 1973
Replaced by *Honeysuckle* 1983
Original illustration Thomas Green c1824

Arctotis Grandiflora – (6) African Daisy
Introduced 1973
Replaced by *Shrubby Peony* 1990
The same illustration was used to create the *Treasure Flower* in 1985 by changing the colour from orange to pink and adding more flower heads, the two co-existed for four years.
Original illustration Thomas Green, c1824

Lonicera Periclymenum – Honeysuckle
Introduced 1983
Replacing *Manchineel Tree*
Colours changed from orange and red to peach and yellow in 1994
Replaced by *Lily Flowered Azalea* 1999
Original illustration William Clarke, 1835

Helleborus Niger – Christmas Rose
Introduced 1984 – still available
Replacing *Yellow Crown Imperial*
Original illustration Stevenson and Churchill

Paeonia Moutan – Shrubby Peony
Introduced 1990 – still available
Replacing *African Daisy*
Original illustration William Clarke c1825

Chrysanthemum Coccineum – Flowered Chrysanthemum
Introduced 1994 – still available
Replacing *Mexican Lily*
Original illustration William Curtis, 1792

Clematis Florida – Virgins Bower
Introduced 1995 – still available
Replacing *Venus' Fly Trap*
Original illustration from *The Botanists Repository, Vol VI*

Rhododendrum Liliiflorum – Lily Flowered Azalea
Introduced 1999 – still available
Replacing *Honeysuckle*

8-inch Side Plates and 13-inch Steak Plates

Cucurbita Citrullus – (1) Water Melon
Introduced 1973
Replaced by *Purple Rock Rose* 1980
Original illustration Thomas Green c1824

Hyacinthus Orientalis – (2) Oriental Hyacinth
Introduced 1973 became Eastern Hyacinth in 1985 – still available
The *Oriental Hyacinth* was the same flower but in white and green.
Original illustration Thomas Green c1824

Solanum Dulcamara – (3) Woody Nightshade
Introduced 1973
Replaced by *Sweet William* 1994
The original version of the Nightshade motif featured a blue bee which was replaced in the 1980s by a moth.
Original illustration William Clarke, 1835

Capsicum Rubrum – (4) Red Peppers
Introduced 1973
Replaced by *Aquilegia* 1984
Original illustration Thomas Green, c1824

Rosa Canina – (5) Dog Rose
Introduced 1973 – still available
Original illustration William Clarke, 1835

Cactus Grandiflorus – (6) Night Flowering Cereus
Introduced 1973
Replaced by *Treasure Flower* 1985
Original illustration Thomas Green, c1824

Cistus Purpureus – Purple Rock Rose
Introduced 1980 – still available
Replacing *Water Melon* in 1980
Originally had two light pink flower heads, in 1986 this was modified to one light and one dark flower head.
Original illustration Thomas Green, c1824

Aquilegia Gracilis – Slender Columbine
Introduced 1984
Replaced by *Garden Lilac* 1999
Replacing *Capsicum*
Butterflies changed in 1990
Original illustration William Clarke, 1830

Gazania Ringens – Treasure Flower
Introduced 1985 – still available
Replacing *Night Flowering Cereus*
Original illustration Thomas Green, c1824

Dianthus Borrbatus – Sweet William
Introduced 1994
Replacing *Woody Nightshade*
Original illustration William Curtis, 1792

Syringa Vulgaris – Garden Lilac
Introduced 1999
Replacing *Slender Columbine*

6-inch Bread and Butter Plates

Bellis Perennis – (1) Daisy
Introduced 1972 – still available
Original illustration William Clarke, 1835

Aloe – (2) Barbadoes Aloe
Introduced 1972
Replaced by *Cotton Flower* 1976
Original illustration Thomas Green, c1824

Convolvulus – (3) Trailing Bindweed
Introduced 1972 – still available
Butterflies repositioned 1994
Original illustration Thomas Green, c1824

Citrus Medica – (4) Citron
Introduced 1972
Replaced by *Crocus and Snowdrop* 1980
Original illustration Thomas Green, c1824

Cistaceae – (5) Spanish Gum Cistus
Known as *White Cistus* after 1985 when used as an un-named motif to decorate items such as the ten-inch Serif vase and large tureen

Introduced 1972
Replaced by *Cyclamen* on 6-inch plates 1985
Original illustration Thomas Green, c1824

Colchicum – (6) *Meadow Saffron*
Introduced 1972
Replaced by *Small Narcissus* 1995
Original illustration Thomas Green, c1824

Narcissus Minimus – Small Narcissus
Introduced 1995 – still available
Replacing *Meadow Saffron*
Original illustration *The Botanical Magazine*

Galanthus and Crocus – Snowdrop and Crocus
Introduced 1980
Replacing *Citron*
Replaced by *Blue Primrose* in 1999
Original illustration *The Romance of Flowers*, by Louisa Twamley, c1830

Primula Villosa – Blue Primrose
Introduced 1999 – still available
Replaced *Snowdrop and Crocus*
Original illustration unknown

See also (7) *Barbados Cotton Flower*, (8) *Spring Gentian* and *Rhododendron*.

Oatmeal Motifs

The original six oatmeal motifs included four from *La Flore des Dames*. Featured posies rather than singular botanical illustrations and did not include Latin names unlike the other flowers which make up *Botanic Garden*. They were thought to be of a lesser quality than the other motifs and were replaced in 1978 by a mixture of *Speedwell* and 8-inch and 6-inch plate motifs. Remaining transfer stocks were used to decorate the ceramic store jar lids available in the early 1980s.

(1) *Purple Iris*
Introduced 1972 – withdrawn 1978
Original illustration A. Jacquemart, 1840

(2) *Orchid*
Introduced 1972 – withdrawn 1978
Original illustration A. Jacquemart, 1840

(3) *Cyclamen Repandum – Cyclamen*
Introduced 1972 as oatmeal motif only
Replaced *Spanish Gum Cistus* 1985, on 6-inch plate

(4) *Gossypium Barbadense – Barbados Cotton Flower*
Introduced 1972 as an oatmeal decoration
Replaced by *Aloe* 1976, as a 6-inch plate
Withdrawn 1988
Replaced by *Rhododendron*

(5) *Orange Cactus*
Introduced 1972 – withdrawn 1978
Original illustration A. Jacquemart, 1840

(6) *Canterbury Bell* or *Redstar*
Introduced 1972 – withdrawn 1978
Original illustration A. Jacquemart, 1840

Polygala Chamaebuxus – Box Leaved Milkwort
Introduced 1999 – still available

Cups and Saucers Motifs

Myosotis Palustris – Forget-Me-Not
Introduced 1972 – still available
Original illustration William Clarke, 1835

Potentilla Erecta – Common Tormentil
Introduced 1972 – still available on ramekins and eggcups
Replaced by *Broom* on teacups, 1985
Original illustration Thomas Green, c1824

Veronica Chamaedrys – Speedwell
Introduced 1972 – still available
Original illustration William Clarke, 1835

Rhododendron Lepidotum – Rhododendron
Introduced 1972 – still available
Replaced *Cotton Flower* on 6-inch plate, 1988
Original illustration William Clarke, 1835

Viola Tricolor – Heartsease
Introduced 1972 – still available
Original illustration William Clarke, 1835

Angallis Arvensis – Pimpemel
Introduced 1972 – still available
Originally scarlet, changed to dark burgundy in 1993 and then to light and dark pink in the same year.
Original illustration William Clarke, 1835

Cytisus Scoparius – Broom
Introduced 1985
Replacing Tomentil on teacups
Replaced by *Yellow Jasmine* 1999
Original illustration William Clarke, 1835

Jasminum Revolutum - Yellow Jasmine
Introduced 1999 – still available
Replaced *Broom*

Miscellaneous

Camelia Japonica – Double Camelia
Introduced 1991 – withdrawn 1993
Decorated medium lasagne dish only.
Original illustration *Botanist Repository*

Lilium Martagum – Austrian Lily
Introduced 1990 – withdrawn 1993
Decorated large serving and lasagne dishes only.
Replaced by *Clematis*
Original illustration *Botanist Repository*

Gentian Verna – Spring Gentian
Introduced 1972
Replaced by *Rhododendron* on milk jug and *Forget-Me-Not* on the cream jug, c1985
Original illustration Thomas Green, c1824

Arbutus – Strawberry Tree
Introduced 1973 – withdrawn c1983
Un-named designs used to decorate tureen lids

Yellow Foxglove
Introduced 1973 – withdrawn c1983
Un-named designs used to decorate tureen lids, also found on planters

Serif shape. *From top left: teapot, vegetable dish, teacup/saucer, cream soup/stand, coffee pot, meat dish, beaker/saucer, covered scallop, cream jug, sauceboat/stand, covered/open sugar, plate, coffee cup/saucer, bowl.*

Cylinder shape. *From top left: teapot, covered/open sugar, plate, sifter, coffee pot, cream jug, covered scallop, store jar, covered jug, vegetable dish, soup goblet, airtight jar, teacup/saucer, sauceboat/stand, tureen, Cylinder jug, coffee cup/saucer, oval platter, bottle, cheese dish, mug, cream soup/stand, cruet, bowl.*

Meridian shape

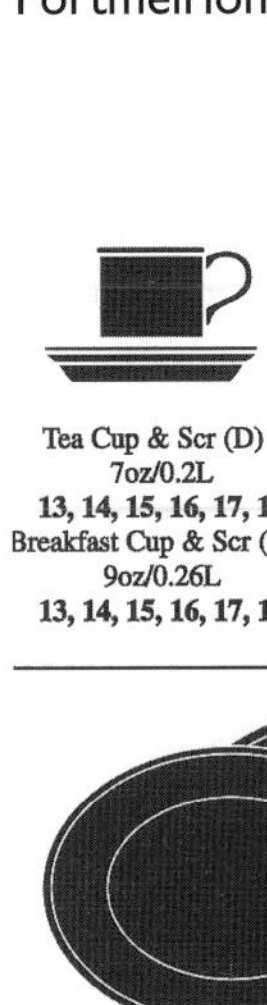
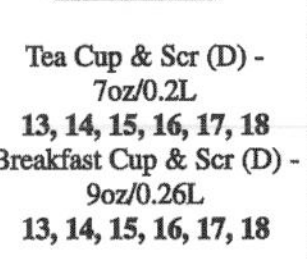
Tea Cup & Scr (D) - 7oz/0.2L
13, 14, 15, 16, 17, 18
Breakfast Cup & Scr (D) - 9oz/0.26L
13, 14, 15, 16, 17, 18

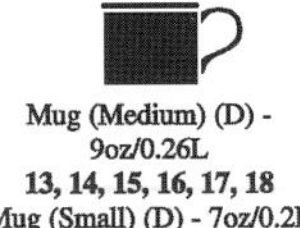
Mug (Medium) (D) - 9oz/0.26L
13, 14, 15, 16, 17, 18
Mug (Small) (D) - 7oz/0.2L
13, 14, 15, 16, 17, 18

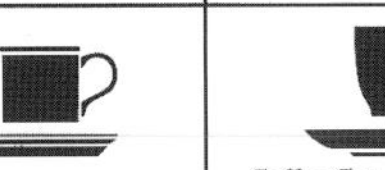
Coffee Mocha & Scr (D) - 4oz/0.1L
13, 14, 15, 16, 17, 18

Espresso Cup & Scr (T) - 2.5oz/0.07L
13, 14, 15, 16, 17, 18

Coffee Cup & Scr (T) - 4oz/0.1L
13, 14, 15, 16, 17, 18

Tea Cup & Scr (T) - 7oz/0.2L
13, 14, 15, 16, 17, 18
Breakfast Cup & Scr (T) - 10oz/0.28L
13, 14, 15, 16, 17, 18

Jumbo Cup & Saucer - 20oz/0.6L
7, 10, 13, 16, 17, 18

Bristol Tankard - 14oz/0.4L
7, 10, 13, 16, 17, 18

Bell Beaker - 10oz/0.28L
7, 10, 13, 16, 17, 18

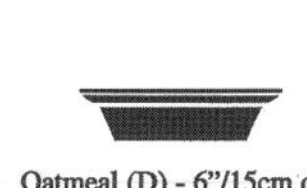
Oatmeal (D) - 6"/15cm d.
7, 10, 13, 16, 17, 18

Delft Mug - 12oz/0.35L
7, 10, 13, 16, 17, 18

Coffee Mug - 0.5pt/0.28L
7, 10, 13, 16, 17, 18

Breakfast Mug - 9oz/0.26L
7, 10, 13, 16, 17, 18

Soup Plate (D) - 8"/20cm d.
7, 8, 9, 10, 11, 12

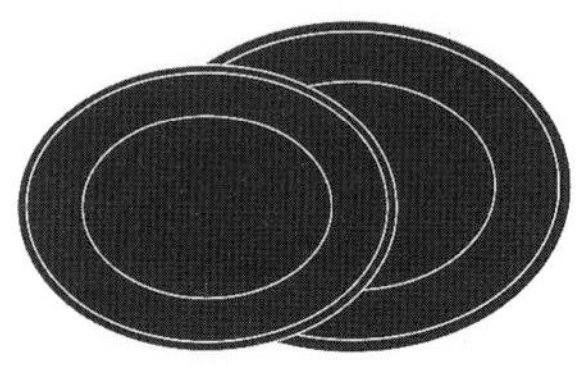

Oval Steak Platter - 11"/28cm **20, 21, 22, 23, 24, 25**
Oval Steak Platter - 13"/33cm **1, 2, 3, 4, 5, 6**

Plate (D) - 6"/15cm d. **7, 8, 9, 10, 11, 12**
Plate (D) - 8"/20cm d. **20, 21, 22, 23, 24, 25**
Plate (D) - 10"/25cm d. **1, 2, 3, 4, 5, 6**

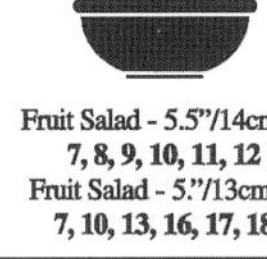
Fruit Salad - 5.5"/14cm d.
7, 8, 9, 10, 11, 12
Fruit Salad - 5."/13cm d.
7, 10, 13, 16, 17, 18

Sugar (R) - 3.25"/8cm d.
Cov. Sugar (R) - 3.25"/8cm d.
7

Sugar (D) - 3.25"/8cm d.
Cov. Sugar (D) - 3.25"/8cm d.
7

Cream (R) - 12oz/0.35L
13

Low Pasta Bowl - 8"/20cm d.
20, 21, 22, 23, 24, 25

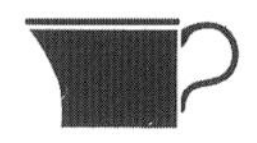
Cream (Small) (D) - 7oz/0.2L **18**

Milk Jug (R) - 1pt/0.5L
16

Tea Pot (R) - 2pt/1.1L - **24**
Tea Pot (R) - 1pt/0.5L - **10**
Tea Pot (R) - 7oz/0.2L
7, 10, 13, 16, 17, 18

Coffee Pot (R) - 2.75pt/1.5L
6

Cafetière - 28oz/0.8L
22
Lidded Jug - 28oz/0.8L
22

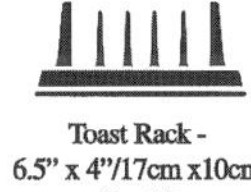
Toast Rack - 6.5" x 4"/17cm x10cm
7 + 10

Covered Buttered Dish (Oblong) - 6" x 3"/15cm x 8cm
12 + 18 (Base - **7**)
Covered Butter Dish (Square) - 5.5" x 4.5"/14cm x 11cm
10 + 18 (Base - **7**)

Conserve/Marmalade Jar - 3.25"/8cm d.
7

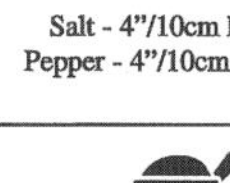
Salt - 4"/10cm h. - **7**
Pepper - 4"/10cm h. - **10**

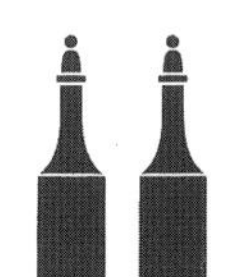
Oil - 8.5"/22cm h.
13
Vinegar - 8.5"/22cm h.
16

Parmesan Pot - 5"/13cm d.
13

Mustard Pot with Spoon - 2.5"/6cm d.
13

Gravy Boat & Stand (R) - 20oz/0.6L
16

2 Tier Cake Stand - (Plate - 10"/25cm d. - **4**) (Plate - 8"/20cm d. - **24**)

Fruit Drainer & Stand - 4"/10cm h.
7 + 10 + 13 + 16 + 17 +18

Cheese Dome - 11"28cm d. (Base) - (Base - **4**) (Lid - **7 +10**)

Soup Tureen & Lid - 8pt/4.4L
(Base - **6 + 3**) (Lid - **17**)

Soup Tureen Ladle - 7oz/0.2L
7 + 12

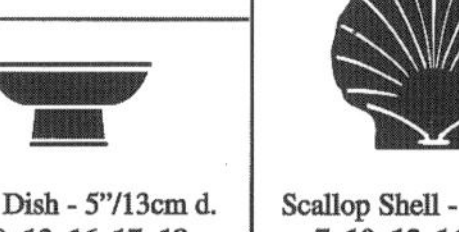
Sorbet Dish - 5"/13cm d.
7, 10, 13, 16, 17, 18

Scallop Shell - 4.5"/11
7, 10, 13, 16, 17, 18
(Pack of 4)

Flan Dish - 10" d. - **B**
Flan Dish - 8"/20cm d. **F**

Pizza Plate - 12"/30cm d. **K**
Pizza Plate - 10"/25cm d. **B**

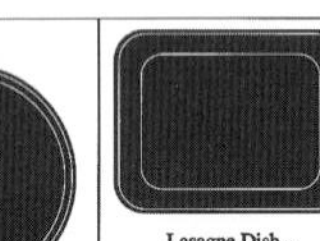
Lasagne Dish - 15" x 11"/38cm x 28cm - **F**
Lasagne Dish - 12.5" x 10"/32cm x 25cm - **B**
Lasagne Dish - 9" x 7"/23cm x 18cm - **G**

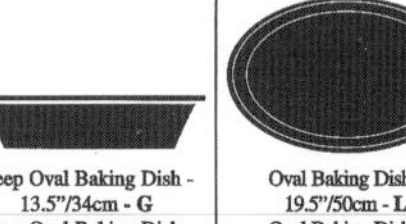
Deep Oval Baking Dish - 13.5"/34cm - **G**
Deep Oval Baking Dish - 11"/28cm - **A**
Deep Oval Baking Dish - 8"/20cm
A, B, C, D, E, F

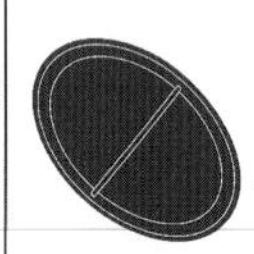
Oval Baking Dish - 19.5"/50cm - **L**
Oval Baking Dish - 16"/41cm - **F**
Oval Baking Dish - 14.5"/37cm - **G**
Oval Baking Dish - 11.5"/29cm - **F**

Oval Divided Dish - 11.5"/29cm
B + G

Romantic Water Jug - 3.75pt/2.1L - **L**
Romantic Water Jug - 1.75pt/1L - **B**
Romantic Water Jug - 0.75pt/0.4L - **E**

Staffordshire Jug - 2pt/1.35L
H
Staffordshire Jug - 1pt/0.5L
A, B, C, D, E, F
Staffordshire Jug - 0.5pt/0.3L
A, B, C, D, E, F

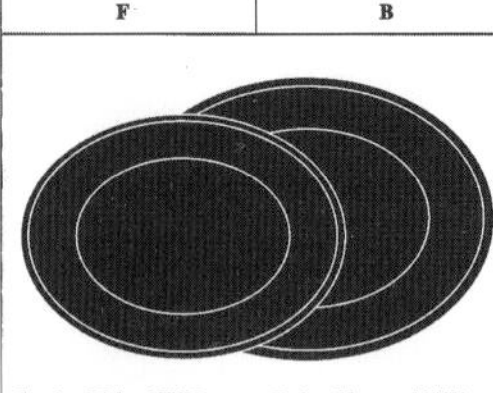
Serving Dish - 15"/38cm
K

Turkey Platter - 20"/51cm
F + H

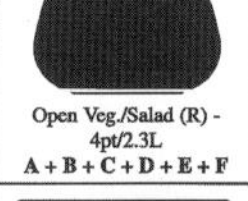
Open Veg./Salad (R) - 4pt/2.3L
A + B + C + D + E + F

Open Veg, Dish/Souffle (D) - 3pt/2L -
A + B + C + D + E + F

Cov. Veg. Dish Casserole (D) - 3pt/1.7L -
A + B + C + D + E + F

Cov. Casserole (R) - 4pt/2.3L
B + G
(Lid - **A + D**)

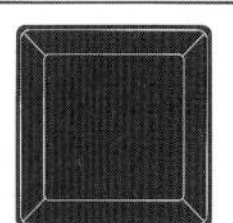
Deep Square Dish - 10"25cm
F

Sweet Dish - 4.5"/11cm d.
A, B, C, D, E, F

Tea Bag /Spoon Rest - 5.5"/14cm w. - **A, B, C, D, E, F**

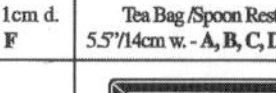

Scented Candle - 2.5"/6cm h.
A, B, C, D, E, F

Trinket Tray - 7.5" x 4.5"/19cm x 11cm. - **F**

Individual Casserole (D) - 16oz/0.45L
A, B, C, D, E, F

Ramekin - (Set of 6) 5oz/0.15L
H

Crescent Dish - 9"/23cm w.
A, B, C, D, E, F

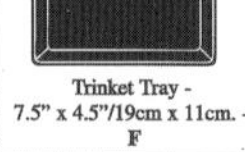
Oval Gratin Dish - 23cm/9"
B

Oval Gratin Dish - 29cm/11.5"
L

Oval Gratin Dish - 33cm/113"
F

Candlestick - 9"/23cm h.
H

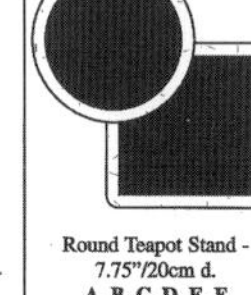
Round Teapot Stand - 7.75"/20cm d.
A, B, C, D, E, F
Square Teapot Stand - 7.75"/20cm
A, B, C, D, E, F

Pomona - Kitchenware

Utensil Jar - 6.5"/16cm h. -
A, B, C, D, E, F
Utensil Jar - 5.25"/13cm h. -
A, B, C, D, E, F

Airtight Jar - 8"/20cm h. -
A, B, C, D, E, F
Airtight Jar - 7"/18cm h. -
A, B, C, D, E, F
Airtight Jar - 5.5"/14cm h. -
A, B, C, D, E, F
Airtight Jar - 4"/10cm h. -
A, B, C, D, E, F
Spice Jar - 2.5"/6cm h. - **A, B, C, D, E, F**

Spaghetti Jar - 11.5"/29cm h.
L

Pudding Basin - 1.5pt/0.8L
A + B + C + D + E + F

Store Crock - 9"/23cm h.
L
Store Crock - 7"/18cm h.
A, B, C, D, E, F

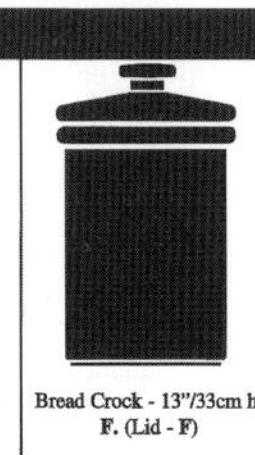
Bread Crock - 13"/33cm h.
F. (Lid - **F**)

Pomona - Mini Giftware

Staffordshire Jug - 3"/8cm h.

Selection of **Botanic Garden** *tableware, serving pieces, cookware, giftware and kitchenware.*

BACKSTAMPS

1931-61: Often covering Johnson, Lancaster & Sandland marks

1960-62: Often covering Johnson, Lancaster & Sandland Marks

1960-62: Versions also found on Moss Agate, Dolphin and Tiger Lily

Old Staffordshire
Porcelains
KIRKHAM 1858
ENGLAND

1946-1961: 'Old Staffordshire' backstamp on Chickens and Antique Jugs

1962-Present: General backstamp, colours vary, green and yellow versions used on shape seconds

c1962-1966: On Kirkham shapes and where room for Portmeirion backstamp is limited

1962-75: Rubber stamp mainly found with black and white printed pots

1962-75: Versions also found on Totem and other embossed ranges

1962-77: Oval format includes pattern name, colours vary

1962-77: For smaller items, mark includes pattern name, colours vary

1962-69: Embossed mark found on Totem shapes

1964-68: Embossed mark, versions also found on Totem and other embossed ranges

1965: One of six distinctive marks for Gold- Check, Flame, Rule, Section, Sign and Signal

1966-77: Portmeirion omitted from this backstamp

1966-74: Magic City (1966-74) with stamp required for export to Irish Republic (c1970)

1968-70: Backstamp may include pattern name, Cuffley's name omitted later

1970-75: On commemorative items commissioned by Hugh Foulerton, also with Portmeirion Pottery Ltd.

1971-83: Embossed mark for the Meridian shape

c1970-72: On a variety of sepia and black on white motifs exclusive to Chaumette in France

1972-77: Mark on smaller items, larger marks include names of the sea creatures pictured

1970-77: Originally used on 'Year Tankards', later on more general commemoratives

c1972: Original large stamp without designer's name

1972-82: With designer's name

c1975-82: With designer's name. From 1982 a tiny '8' and '2' in blank area below 'MEI' of the world Portmeirion. Examples with '8' and '4' are known, but rare.

1970-1983: On SWE designs, stamped gold on matt black 'SH' appears after 1976

1975-83: Embossed mark also includes size numbers 1-3

1978-82: On all seconds items decorated in Wales

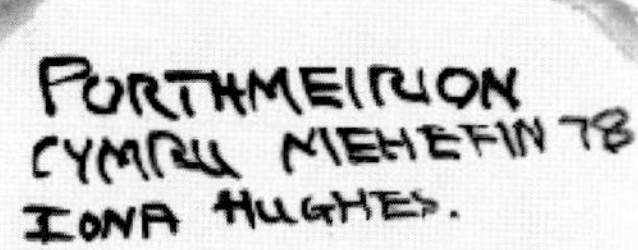

1978: Handpainted in Wales by Iona Hughes

1980-1999: Originally in brown, c1985 in red

Weeping Hearts 1986. One of many attractive pattern marks found in the 1970s-80s

1984-1990: Original mark on 'Parianware'

1989-Present: Embossed mark on 'antique Parianware'

1994-1999: Portmeirion China, includes name of pattern and designer

1993-Present: On items available exclusively to Collectors' Club members

1970-Present: Many versions, includes name of pattern and designer on National Trust commissions

c1980: Gold stamp mark on oven-to-table stoneware

1993-1997: Portmeirion Studio, includes name of handpainted pattern

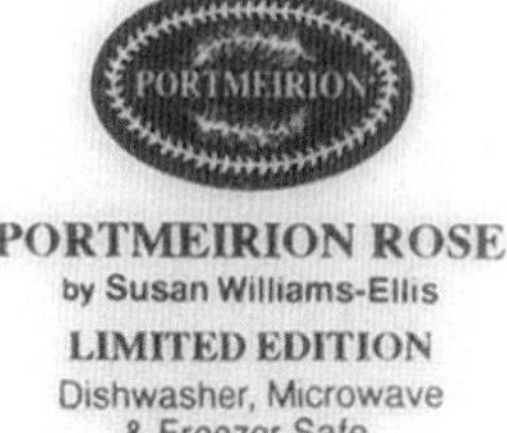

1999-Present: This new oval design replaces the individual backstamps previously used on Botanic Garden and Pomona etc. Pattern names are printed as shown.

2000: Bespoke mark designed for specially commissioned items. This, for The Prisoner shop in Portmeirion village.